BFF

Best Friends Forever

By Isabel & Emily Lluch

Have fun, share and laugh while
getting to know your best friends!

WS Publishing Group
www.WSPublishingGroup.com
San Diego, California 92119

CHOOSE

This is BFF:
Best Friends Forever,
the perfect book of questions
and quizzes for girls!

Here's what to do:
Get up to three of your best friends to fill it
out with you. Each of you should choose the
symbol you want to be yours throughout the
book. Fill out the pages with your names,
personal info, and mottos to make the book
your own.

Now bring BFF to sleepovers, pass it
around at lunch, do it after school, or
bring it on the bus to your next soccer
game.

Answer the questions and take the
quizzes at your own pace. With hundreds
of questions about crushes, school,
family, likes and dislikes, travel, dreams,
and funny scenarios, they'll be plenty to
keep you laughing.

You won't believe what you
learn about your best friends
that you never knew!

name

YOUR SYMBOL ...

name

name

name

Words that describe me:

66   99

Place a favorite
photo of you here.

Name: .... Age: ....

Hobbies:...

....

My motto: ....

....

....

....

Words that describe me:

" "

Place a favorite
photo of you here.

Name: .... Age: ....

Hobbies:...

....

My motto: ....

....

....

....

Words that describe me:

" "

Place a favorite
photo of you here.

Name: .... Age: ....

Hobbies:..

....

My motto: ....

....

....

....

Words that describe me:

" "

Place a favorite
photo of you here.

Name: .... Age: ....

Hobbies:...

....

My motto: ....

....

....

....

Birth **month**

✌️ .... 🌸 .... 👄 .... 💘 ....

Fav **color**

✌️ .... 🌸 .... 👄 .... 💘 ....

One *food* you could eat every day

✌️ .... 🌸 .... 👄 .... 💘 ....

Last person you TEXTED

✌️ .... 🌸 .... 👄 .... 💘 ....

Favorite *emoticon*

✌️ .... 🌸 .... 👄 .... 💘 ....

You'd **never** be caught DEAD wearing …

✌️ .... 🌸 .... 👄 .... 💘 ....

Ever **ditched** class?

✌️ .... 🌸 .... 👄 .... 💘 ....

If **yes**, what did you do?

✌️ .... 🌸 .... 👄 .... 💘 ....

Best thing about your **crush**

✌️ .... 🌸 .... 👄 .... 💘 ....

Hug or handshake?

✌️ .... 🌸 .... 👄 .... 💘 ....

Best **friend** right now

✌ .... ❀ .... 👄 .... ♡ ....

Work at a *SUMMER CAMP* or make drinks at **Starbucks**?

✌ .... ❀ .... 👄 .... ♡ ....

Last **WEBSITE** you went on

✌ .... ❀ .... 👄 .... ♡ ....

Blind or **deaf**?

✌ .... ❀ .... 👄 .... ♡ ....

Ever **swam** in your underwear?

✌ .... ❀ .... 👄 .... ♡ ....

Sushi: Love it, Hate it, or Just OK?

✌ .... ❀ .... 👄 .... ♡ ....

Waffles or pancakes

✌ .... ❀ .... 👄 .... ♡ ....

Person to your **left**

✌ .... ❀ .... 👄 .... ♡ ....

Word that makes your skin **CRAWL**

✌ .... ❀ .... 👄 .... ♡ ....

Fav flavor of frozen yogurt

✌ .... ❀ .... 👄 .... ♡ ....

Coffee: Smells good, Tastes good, or Gives you bad breath?

✌ .... ✿ .... 👄 .... ♡ ....

WORST class in school

✌ .... ✿ .... 👄 .... ♡ ....

Coolest class in school

✌ .... ✿ .... 👄 .... ♡ ....

Front of the bus or **back** of the bus?

✌ .... ✿ .... 👄 .... ♡ ....

Skiing or **snowboarding**?

✌ .... ✿ .... 👄 .... ♡ ....

Fav *technology*

✌ .... ✿ .... 👄 .... ♡ ....

Who was your first **kiss**?

✌ .... ✿ .... 👄 .... ♡ ....

One **word** to describe it

✌ .... ✿ .... 👄 .... ♡ ....

Ever been in a **FIGHT**?

✌ .... ✿ .... 👄 .... ♡ ....

If **YES**, with who?

✌ .... ✿ .... 👄 .... ♡ ....

More embarrassing: Dog poop on your shoe or Gum in your hair?

✌ .... ✿ .... 👄 .... 💘 ....

Best way to make some extra *cash $$$$*

✌ .... ✿ .... 👄 .... 💘 ....

Most **annoying** rule at your house

✌ .... ✿ .... 👄 .... 💘 ....

SCARIEST movie ever

✌ .... ✿ .... 👄 .... 💘 ....

One thing that makes you *feel better* after a bad day

✌ .... ✿ .... 👄 .... 💘 ....

A world without TV: OMG, no! or Wouldn't miss it.

✌ .... ✿ .... 👄 .... 💘 ....

Diamonds or **pearls**?

✌ .... ✿ .... 👄 .... 💘 ....

What country are your ancestors from?

✌ .... ✿ .... 👄 .... 💘 ....

PDA: Tacky, Cute, or You're just jealous?

✌ .... ✿ .... 👄 .... 💘 ....

Rate how *smart* you are on a scale of 1 to 10

✌ .... ✿ .... 👄 .... 💘 ....

What's your CURFEW?

✌ .... ❀ .... 👄 .... 💘 ....

Dream car

✌ .... ❀ .... 👄 .... 💘 ....

Your **parents** are …

✌ .... ❀ .... 👄 .... 💘 ....

You can choose one **designer** to dress you every day: Who do you pick?

✌ .... ❀ .... 👄 .... 💘 ....

Your ex: Still friends or Hate his guts?

✌ .... ❀ .... 👄 .... 💘 ....

Fake eyelashes or red lipstick?

✌ .... ❀ .... 👄 .... 💘 ....

Ever thrown water balloons?

✌ .... ❀ .... 👄 .... 💘 ....

At WHO?

✌ .... ❀ .... 👄 .... 💘 ....

Caught **snowflakes** on your tongue?

✌ .... ❀ .... 👄 .... 💘 ....

Biggest **celeb** crush

✌ .... ❀ .... 👄 .... 💘 ....

Popcorn or **candy** at the movies?

✌ .... ✿ .... 👄 .... ♡ ....

Make a **little money** at a job you **love** or make a **lot of money** at a job you **hate**?

✌ .... ✿ .... 👄 .... ♡ ....

Brains or *beauty*?

✌ .... ✿ .... 👄 .... ♡ ....

Last *cute* guy you talked to.

✌ .... ✿ .... 👄 .... ♡ ....

Brad Pitt or **George Clooney**?

✌ .... ✿ .... 👄 .... ♡ ....

UGG boots: Still cute or Over 'em?

✌ .... ✿ .... 👄 .... ♡ ....

CHINESE food or Mexican?

✌ .... ✿ .... 👄 .... ♡ ....

Golf: Really hard, Really fun, or Really boring?

✌ .... ✿ .... 👄 .... ♡ ....

NIGHT OWL or EARLY BIRD?

✌ .... ✿ .... 👄 .... ♡ ....

Ever WON a spelling bee?

✌ .... ✿ .... 👄 .... ♡ ....

Been in a **play**?

✌ .... ✿ .... 👄 .... 💘 ....

KISSED a friend's crush?

✌ .... ✿ .... 👄 .... 💘 ....

Rate how much of a **gossip** you are on a scale of **1** to **10**

✌ .... ✿ .... 👄 .... 💘 ....

Gotten an **F**?

✌ .... ✿ .... 👄 .... 💘 ....

In what **subject**?

✌ .... ✿ .... 👄 .... 💘 ....

Fav 4-letter word (doesn't have to be a bad word!)

✌ .... ✿ .... 👄 .... 💘 ....

Ice cream flavor: chocolate, mint chip, or cookie dough?

✌ .... ✿ .... 👄 .... 💘 ....

Curly or STRAIGHT?

✌ .... ✿ .... 👄 .... 💘 ....

First thing **on your mind** this morning

✌ .... ✿ .... 👄 .... 💘 ....

Ever lost something?

✌ .... ✿ .... 👄 .... 💘 ....

Right now: sleepy, hungry, cranky, or happy?

✌ .... ❀ .... 👄 .... 💘 ....

When is the next time you'll **see your crush**?

✌ .... ❀ .... 👄 .... 💘 ....

Jeans or dress?

✌ .... ❀ .... 👄 .... 💘 ....

Silver or gold jewelry?

✌ .... ❀ .... 👄 .... 💘 ....

Baseball hats: Cute on girls or Only on guys?

✌ .... ❀ .... 👄 .... 💘 ....

Motorcycles: Cool or way dangerous?

✌ .... ❀ .... 👄 .... 💘 ....

Who would be your dream prom date?

✌ .... ❀ .... 👄 .... 💘 ....

Worst pain you've ever felt

✌ .... ❀ .... 👄 .... 💘 ....

Flower you'd like a bouquet of

✌ .... ❀ .... 👄 .... 💘 ....

Most **quotable** movie

✌ .... ❀ ....

👄 .... 💘 ....

Quiz:

What's Your Guy Grade?

1. Your crush stays home sick from school. You:

a. Show up at his house with a movie, his homework, chicken soup, and hot tea.
b. Send him a "get well soon" text with a smiley face.
c. Figure you'll see him at school when he's better.

✌ .... ✽ .... 👄 .... 💘 ....

2. You've been hanging out with a cute guy for a few weeks. When he calls, you:

a. Talk to him for over an hour.
b. Chat about your day, then tell him you'll see him tomorrow.
c. Get quiet; you never know what to say on the phone.

✌ .... ✽ .... 👄 .... 💘 ....

3. Your guy plans a poker night with his friends, so you:

a. Call him a couple times, just to check in.
b. Have your girls over to watch movies.
c. Feel bummed out that he's busy.

✌ .... ✽ .... 👄 .... 💘 ....

4. You suspect a girl in your art class has a thing for your guy. The next time you're with him and she walks by, you:

a. Grab him and start making out. Now she'll know he's yours.
b. Smile. She'll get how happy you guys are together.
c. Feel super awkward and stare at your shoes.

✌ .... ❀ .... 👄 .... 🏹 ....

5. There's a new chick flick out that you want to see, but your boy isn't into it. You:

a. Drag him to the movie anyway. If he really cares about you, he'll suffer through it.
b. Promise you'll go to the horror movie he wants to see next week if he comes with you.
c. Skip the movie and stay in playing video games at his house.

✌ .... ❀ .... 👄 .... 🏹 ....

6. Your guy needs a bit of help in the fashion department; what's your approach?

a. Show up at his house with a trash bag, then take him to the mall so you can pick out new clothes for him.
b. Be sure to give him lots of compliments when he wears a cute outfit, so he knows what he looks the best in.
c. Stew silently when he shows up for dinner at your house in a holey T-shirt.

✌ .... ❀ .... 👄 .... 🏹 ....

7. The cute new guy at your youth group asks you if you want to hang out this weekend, and you exchange phone numbers. You:

a. Call him that night to see what he has planned for your date.
b. Shoot him a text in a few days to see if he wants to meet up.
c. Wait to hear from him.

....

8. Your guy cancels plans with you at the last minute to go on a fishing trip. When he calls to apologize, you:

a. Ignore his call. He's in the dog house for sure.
b. Say you are hurt and you'd like it if he made it up to you.
c. Say, "That's OK, no problem." You like to seem easy-going.

....

9. While you are in the car with your boy, you always:

a. Change the radio station, talk about your day, and remind him where to turn.
b. Sing along to the song that's on.
c. Hope he knows where he's going. You don't want to be a backseat driver.

....

10. You see your guy talking with his team after school. You:

a. Step right into the middle of the group and give him a big hug.
b. Wave and say, "I'll talk to you later."
c. Walk by. You don't want to interrupt him with his buddies.

....

11. Your boyfriend tells you that he's going to be spending the summer with his aunt in London. Your response?

a. "Oh my god, what about me?!"
b. "You're so lucky. I can't wait to see pictures!"
c. "I guess I'll see you in September."

✌ .... ❀ .... 👄 .... ♡ ....

Mostly a's: Grade F. ★

Being pushy or trying to change a guy is a recipe for failure in a relationship. It's good for you and your guy to have your own friends and interests. If you try to change him or take over all his free time, he'll want to get as far away from you as possible.

Mostly b's: Grade A.

You're sweet without being overbearing. When you have a crush on a guy, you let him know you're thinking of him but still leave him wanting more. You also know that compromising — not being bossy — means boyfriend bliss!

Mostly c's: Grade C.

Wake up — no guy likes a girl who's a doormat! You don't speak up enough — maybe because you're shy, or maybe because you don't want to rock the boat — but don't forget, guys like independent girls who go after what they want. If you show him you're fun and happy on your own, he'll know you're a keeper.

Been to a *wedding*?

✌ .... ❀ .... 👄 .... 💘 ....

Gone bowling?

✌ .... ❀ .... 👄 .... 💘 ....

PEANUT BUTTER: Creamy or chunky?

✌ .... ❀ .... 👄 .... 💘 ....

What outfit makes you feel the *cutest*?

✌ .... ❀ .... 👄 .... 💘 ....

Letter grade you're most likely to get

✌ .... ❀ .... 👄 .... 💘 ....

(Blank) are a girl's **best friend**

✌ .... ❀ .... 👄 .... 💘 ....

Rate **chocolate** on a scale of **1** to **10**

✌ .... ❀ .... 👄 .... 💘 ....

Stripes or **polka dots**?

✌ .... ❀ .... 👄 .... 💘 ....

Hug your **dad** in **public**?

✌ .... ❀ .... 👄 .... 💘 ....

RAP music or **COUNTRY**?

✌ .... ❀ .... 👄 .... 💘 ....

You'd be **VOTED** most likely to …

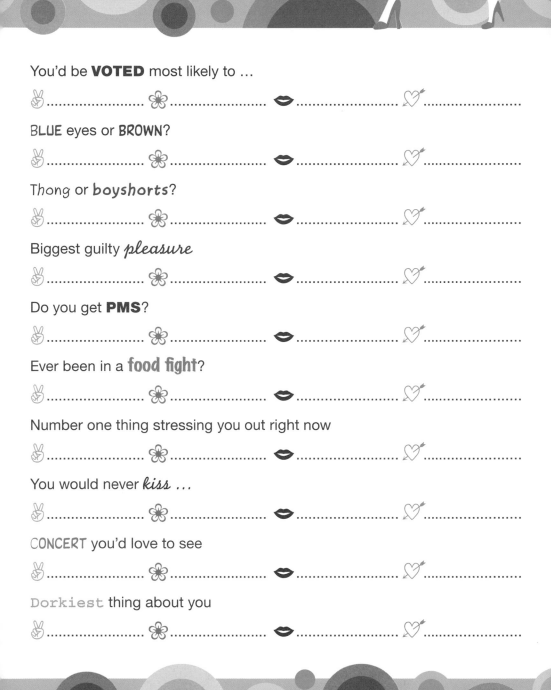

✌ .... ❀ .... 👄 .... ♡ ....

BLUE eyes or BROWN?

✌ .... ❀ .... 👄 .... ♡ ....

Thong or *boyshorts*?

✌ .... ❀ .... 👄 .... ♡ ....

Biggest guilty *pleasure*

✌ .... ❀ .... 👄 .... ♡ ....

Do you get **PMS**?

✌ .... ❀ .... 👄 .... ♡ ....

Ever been in a **food fight**?

✌ .... ❀ .... 👄 .... ♡ ....

Number one thing stressing you out right now

✌ .... ❀ .... 👄 .... ♡ ....

You would never *kiss* …

✌ .... ❀ .... 👄 .... ♡ ....

CONCERT you'd love to see

✌ .... ❀ .... 👄 .... ♡ ....

Dorkiest thing about you

✌ .... ❀ .... 👄 .... ♡ ....

Fav thing about your house

✌ .... ❀ .... 👄 .... 💘 ....

Ever built a **snowman**?

✌ .... ❀ .... 👄 .... 💘 ....

Exotic vacation you would want to take

✌ .... ❀ .... 👄 .... 💘 ....

What was the last thing you got <u>grounded</u> for?

✌ .... ❀ .... 👄 .... 💘 ....

Friend who moved *away* who you *miss*

✌ .... ❀ .... 👄 .... 💘 ....

BIKINI or ONE-PIECE?

✌ .... ❀ .... 👄 .... 💘 ....

Ever had **surgery**?

✌ .... ❀ .... 👄 .... 💘 ....

On what?

✌ .... ❀ .... 👄 .... 💘 ....

Snakes: Cool or slimy?

✌ .... ❀ .... 👄 .... 💘 ....

Fav color pen

✌ .... ❀ .... 👄 .... 💘 ....

FOOTBALL: I don't get it, Fun to watch, or Cute guys?

✌ .... ✿ .... 👄 .... 💘 ....

Ever won an **AWARD?**

✌ .... ✿ .... 👄 .... 💘 ....

What for?

✌ .... ✿ .... 👄 .... 💘 ....

Glasses: Cute or nerdy?

✌ .... ✿ .... 👄 .... 💘 ....

Friend who let you down recently

✌ .... ✿ .... 👄 .... 💘 ....

If you could be one **animal**, what would it be?

✌ .... ✿ .... 👄 .... 💘 ....

Yummiest pizza topping

✌ .... ✿ .... 👄 .... 💘 ....

One thing you **HATE** doing

✌ .... ✿ .... 👄 .... 💘 ....

Best job: Model, actress, or singer?

✌ .... ✿ .... 👄 .... 💘 ....

Better to be an only child or identical twin?

✌ .... ✿ .... 👄 .... 💘 ....

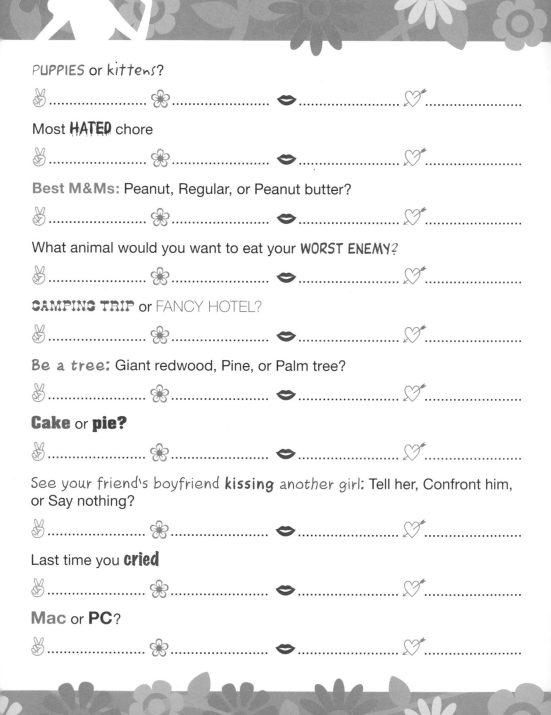

PUPPIES or kittens?

🖐 .... ✿ .... 👄 .... 💘 ....

Most HATED chore

🖐 .... ✿ .... 👄 .... 💘 ....

Best M&Ms: Peanut, Regular, or Peanut butter?

🖐 .... ✿ .... 👄 .... 💘 ....

What animal would you want to eat your WORST ENEMY?

✌ .... ✿ .... 👄 .... 💘 ....

CAMPING TRIP or FANCY HOTEL?

🖐 .... ✿ .... 👄 .... 💘 ....

Be a tree: Giant redwood, Pine, or Palm tree?

🖐 .... ✿ .... 👄 .... 💘 ....

Cake or pie?

✌ .... ✿ .... 👄 .... 💘 ....

See your friend's boyfriend kissing another girl: Tell her, Confront him, or Say nothing?

✌ .... ✿ .... 👄 .... 💘 ....

Last time you cried

🖐 .... ✿ .... 👄 .... 💘 ....

Mac or PC?

✌ .... ✿ .... 👄 .... 💘 ....

PRANK CALLS: Funny or childish?

✌ .... ❀ .... 👄 .... 💘 ....

Rate your *singing voice* on a scale of *1* to *10*

✌ .... ❀ .... 👄 .... 💘 ....

First **R-RATED** movie you ever saw

✌ .... ❀ .... 👄 .... 💘 ....

Lessons you'd want to take: Cooking, Ballroom dancing, Gymnastics, or Ice skating?

✌ .... ❀ .... 👄 .... 💘 ....

RED MEAT: Tasty or gross?

✌ .... ❀ .... 👄 .... 💘 ....

Ever had a **crush** on someone you shouldn't have? **Who?**

✌ .... ❀ .... 👄 .... 💘 ....

Best **present** you ever got

✌ .... ❀ .... 👄 .... 💘 ....

Piercing or *tattoo?*

✌ .... ❀ .... 👄 .... 💘 ....

Ever written a **poem?**

✌ .... ❀ .... 👄 .... 💘 ....

Fav thing about the *girls* in this room

✌ .... ❀ .... 👄 .... 💘 ....

Ever gotten a *surprise party?*

✌ .... ❀ .... 👄 .... 💘 ....

Fav **Disney** movie

✌ .... ❀ .... 👄 .... 💘 ....

Signature perfume

✌ .... ❀ .... 👄 .... 💘 ....

Eaten **crabs** legs?

✌ .... ❀ .... 👄 .... 💘 ....

Sport you wish you did: Surfing, Cheerleading, Soccer, or Softball?

✌ .... ❀ .... 👄 .... 💘 ....

Live in a treehouse or on a houseboat?

✌ .... ❀ .... 👄 .... 💘 ....

Won a **contest?**

✌ .... ❀ .... 👄 .... 💘 ....

For what?

✌ .... ❀ .... 👄 .... 💘 ....

Had your *heart broken?*

✌ .... ❀ .... 👄 .... 💘 ....

Book smarts or **street smarts?**

✌ .... ❀ .... 👄 .... 💘 ....

Fav website

✌ .... ❀ .... 👄 .... 💘 ....

Store in the MALL you could live in

✌ .... ❀ .... 👄 .... 💘 ....

Best bottled water brand

✌ .... ❀ .... 👄 .... 💘 ....

Last time you went down a *waterslide*

✌ .... ❀ .... 👄 .... 💘 ....

Weirdest food you've even eaten

✌ .... ❀ .... 👄 .... 💘 ....

Lost a **bet?**

✌ .... ❀ .... 👄 .... 💘 ....

What did you have **to do?**

✌ .... ❀ .... 👄 .... 💘 ....

Gone *snorkeling?*

✌ .... ❀ .... 👄 .... 💘 ....

Best SUMMER vacation

✌ .... ❀ .... 👄 .... 💘 ....

Love letter or a *dozen roses?*

✌ .... ❀ .... 👄 .... 💘 ....

Been **whitewater** rafting?

✌️ .... 🌸 .... 👄 .... 💘 ....

Black nail polish: Love it or leave it?

✌️ .... 🌸 .... 👄 .... 💘 ....

Marry a *prince* and move to India or *marry* a *janitor* and live in *Beverly Hills*?

✌️ .... 🌸 .... 👄 .... 💘 ....

Girls' roadtrip! Where would you go?

✌️ .... 🌸 .... 👄 .... 💘 ....

Fav brand of *clothing*

✌️ .... 🌸 .... 👄 .... 💘 ....

Ever gotten **detention?**

✌️ .... 🌸 .... 👄 .... 💘 ....

What for?

✌️ .... 🌸 .... 👄 .... 💘 ....

Makeup product you can't live without

✌️ .... 🌸 .... 👄 .... 💘 ....

High heels or *flip-flops*?

✌️ .... 🌸 .... 👄 .... 💘 ....

Get a **mullet** or dye your **hair pink**?

✌️ .... 🌸 .... 👄 .... 💘 ....

Smells better: Fresh-baked cookies or your crush's cologne?

✌ .... ❀ .... 👄 .... 💘 ....

Working out: Awesome, Ugh, or Necessary evil?

✌ .... ❀ .... 👄 .... 💘 ....

Rate how bad you want a boyfriend on a scale of 1 to 10

✌ .... ❀ .... 👄 .... 💘 ....

Where do your *grandparents* live?

✌ .... ❀ .... 👄 .... 💘 ....

Recycling: Gotta do it or Who cares?

✌ .... ❀ .... 👄 .... 💘 ....

Beachy model **waves** or shiny **straight** hair?

✌ .... ❀ .... 👄 .... 💘 ....

Ever **stolen** anything?

✌ .... ❀ .... 👄 .... 💘 ....

WHAT was it?

✌ .... ❀ .... 👄 .... 💘 ....

Did you GET CAUGHT?

✌ .... ❀ .... 👄 .... 💘 ....

One thing you're doing tomorrow

✌ .... ❀ ....

👄 .... 💘 ....

Quiz:

What's Your Workout Personality?

1. What's one of your favorite things about working out?

a. Getting fresh air

b. Ugh, absolutely nothing

c. The rush I get from a great workout sesh

✌ .... ❀ .... 👄 .... 💘 ....

2. What kind of yoga appeals to you the most?

a. Yoga on the beach or a mountain top

b. Sitting and practicing breathing

c. Power yoga that really makes me sweat!

✌ .... ❀ .... 👄 .... 💘 ....

3. If you were to come back as an object in another life, which would you most likely be?

a. Skis

b. Pajamas

c. Running shoes

✌ .... ❀ .... 👄 .... 💘 ....

4. What gear can't you live without?

a. Bike and rollerblades

b. The remote and the Internet

c. Mp3 player and gossip magazines

....

5. Your nickname would be:

a. Nature Girl

b. Sleeping Beauty

c. Cardio Queen

....

6. Best way to spend an hour?

a. Hiking a trail with a friend

b. Watching a reality TV show

c. Hip-hop kickboxing class

....

7. A friend asks you to participate in a 5k Breast Cancer Walk with her. Your first thought is:

a. Awesome, I'm in!

b. Oh no, how far is 5k?

c. I better start training!

....

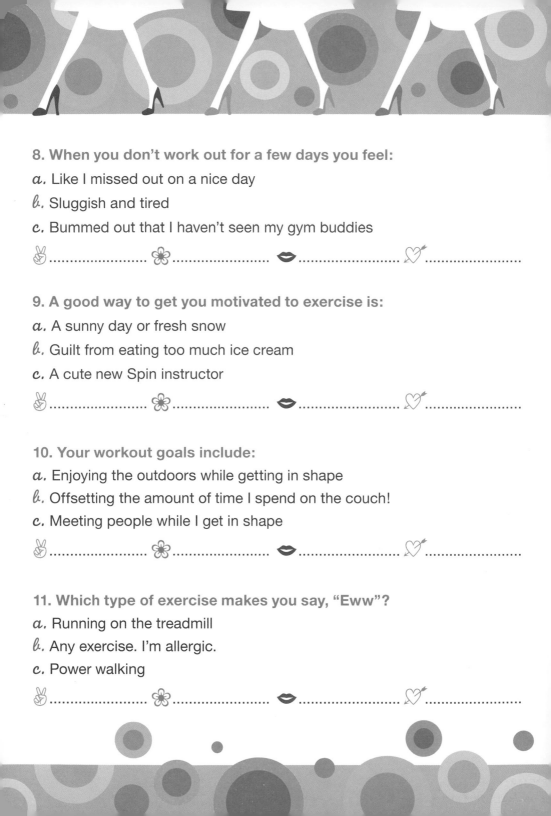

8. When you don't work out for a few days you feel:

a. Like I missed out on a nice day

b. Sluggish and tired

c. Bummed out that I haven't seen my gym buddies

✌ .... ❀ .... 👄 .... 💘 ....

9. A good way to get you motivated to exercise is:

a. A sunny day or fresh snow

b. Guilt from eating too much ice cream

c. A cute new Spin instructor

✌ .... ❀ .... 👄 .... 💘 ....

10. Your workout goals include:

a. Enjoying the outdoors while getting in shape

b. Offsetting the amount of time I spend on the couch!

c. Meeting people while I get in shape

✌ .... ❀ .... 👄 .... 💘 ....

11. Which type of exercise makes you say, "Eww"?

a. Running on the treadmill

b. Any exercise. I'm allergic.

c. Power walking

✌ .... ❀ .... 👄 .... 💘 ....

Mostly a's: Outdoorsy Chick

The gym makes you break out in hives! You'd much rather take your workout outdoors. Try hiking, surfing, rollerblading, snowboarding, rock climbing, or horseback riding. Pretty much any activity you do in nature while getting some fresh air is perfect for you. Better still, invite your friends to join you! Exercising with friends keeps you motivated.

Mostly b's: Channel Surfer

You're missing out on so much by not exercising! Working out gives you energy for the day, de-stresses you, and gets you in shape for bikini season. If you're nervous to join a gym or start a workout program, start small with DVDs you can do at home or call a friend and go for a brisk walk together. Make working out your way to relax, not curling up on the couch.

Mostly c's: Gym Goddess

You're an athlete-type who loves a gym environment where you can take classes, meet people, and get a great workout. You throw on your Mp3 player and crank out a sweaty Spin session, then chat it up with the cute front-desk guys. Just don't forget about all the awesome opportunities for exercise outside! Mix a hike or bike ride into your workout every so often so you're not stuck inside all the time.

Kiss a pig or **HUG** a donkey?

✌ .... ❀ .... 👄 .... 💘 ....

Jelly: Strawberry, blackberry, or grape?

✌ .... ❀ .... 👄 .... 💘 ....

COWBOY HAT or COWBOY BOOTS?

✌ .... ❀ .... 👄 .... 💘 ....

Best birthday accessory: Tiara or feather boa?

✌ .... ❀ .... 👄 .... 💘 ....

Very **WORST THING** about **guys**

✌ .... ❀ .... 👄 .... 💘 ....

Fruit Pebbles or Captain Crunch?

✌ .... ❀ .... 👄 .... 💘 ....

Ever played *Spin* the Bottle?

✌ .... ❀ .... 👄 .... 💘 ....

Who did you have to **kiss?**

✌ .... ❀ .... 👄 .... 💘 ....

Fav book

✌ .... ❀ .... 👄 .... 💘 ....

Seen a **ghost?**

✌ .... ❀ .... 👄 .... 💘 ....

Fav runway model

✌ .... ❀ .... 👄 .... 💘 ....

Ever **swam** with **dolphins**?

✌ .... ❀ .... 👄 .... 💘 ....

What's your lucky charm?

✌ .... ❀ .... 👄 .... 💘 ....

Fav family VACATION

✌ .... ❀ .... 👄 .... 💘 ....

If you could make **one food calorie** and **fat-free**, what would it be?

✌ .... ❀ .... 👄 .... 💘 ....

Being in honors classes: Awesome or dorky?

✌ .... ❀ .... 👄 .... 💘 ....

Would you ever ask a guy out? Totally or No way!

✌ .... ❀ .... 👄 .... 💘 ....

Fav **HALLOWEEN** costume you ever wore

✌ .... ❀ .... 👄 .... 💘 ....

Your crush winks at you: Wink back or look down?

✌ .... ❀ .... 👄 .... 💘 ....

Who was your very first crush?

✌ .... ❀ .... 👄 .... 💘 ....

Biggest regret

✌ .... ✿ .... 👄 .... ♡ ....

What makes you *feel beautiful*?

✌ .... ✿ .... 👄 .... ♡ ....

How many people have you **kissed**?

✌ .... ✿ .... 👄 .... ♡ ....

What food do you crave when you're PMSing?

✌ .... ✿ .... 👄 .... ♡ ....

Ever **traveled** to another country?

✌ .... ✿ .... 👄 .... ♡ ....

Which one?

✌ .... ✿ .... 👄 .... ♡ ....

You can have any **animal as a pet:** What do you choose?

✌ .... ✿ .... 👄 .... ♡ ....

Two **favorite songs** right now

✌ .... ✿ .... 👄 .... ♡ ....

Going to a dance without a date: **Pretty lame** or **Fun** with the girls?

✌ .... ✿ .... 👄 .... ♡ ....

Where do you want to go to **COLLEGE?**

✌ .... ✿ .... 👄 .... ♡ ....

How big of a flirt are you? Rate yourself on a scale of 1 to 10.

....

Ever wanted to be **more than friends** with a guy friend? **Who?**

....

Would you rather wear a **gorilla suit** to school or join the `badminton team`?

....

Fav **holiday**

....

One thing you **wanna do** when **you're older**

....

Falling down the stairs at school: Total humiliation or No biggie?

....

Best song to work out to?

....

What *celeb's closet* would you love to have?

....

Ever had an *embarrassing* or *mean nickname*? What was it?

....

Read minds or be *able to fly*?

....

Guys who love video games: So immature or Super cute?

✌ .... ❀ .... 👄 .... 💘 ....

Lose all your *clothes* in a fire or not be able to wear *makeup* for a year?

✌ .... ❀ .... 👄 .... 💘 ....

Fav FASHION magazine

✌ .... ❀ .... 👄 .... 💘 ....

Celeb you'd take to **Prom**

✌ .... ❀ .... 👄 .... 💘 ....

Share a **room with a sibling** or **live in the attic**?

✌ .... ❀ .... 👄 .... 💘 ....

Best outfit for the *first day of school*

✌ .... ❀ .... 👄 .... 💘 ....

Do you get `allowance`($$$)? How much?

✌ .... ❀ .... 👄 .... 💘 ....

Eat **baby food** or drink *prune juice*?

✌ .... ❀ .... 👄 .... 💘 ....

Blind date: Awesome or FREAKY?

✌ .... ❀ .... 👄 .... 💘 ....

Skydiving: Totally, No way! or Done it?

✌ .... ❀ .... 👄 .... 💘 ....

Best **salty** food

✌ .... ❁ .... 👄 .... 💘 ....

Reality TV: Stupid or Entertaining?

✌ .... ❁ .... 👄 .... 💘 ....

Fav thing to do on a **rainy day**

✌ .... ❁ .... 👄 .... 💘 ....

Your **favorite feature**

✌ .... ❁ .... 👄 .... 💘 ....

Your **least favorite feature**

✌ .... ❁ .... 👄 .... 💘 ....

Rate how well you *keep a secret* on a scale of *1* to *10*

✌ .... ❁ .... 👄 .... 💘 ....

Believe in **aliens**?

✌ .... ❁ .... 👄 .... 💘 ....

Most IRRITATING celebrity

✌ .... ❁ .... 👄 .... 💘 ....

Ever bowled a **strike**?

✌ .... ❁ .... 👄 .... 💘 ....

Ever wear your **dad's socks**?

✌ .... ❁ .... 👄 .... 💘 ....

Miley Cyrus: Love her or Can't stand her?

✌ .... ❀ .... 👄 .... 💘 ....

Ever put **Skittles** in your soda?

✌ .... ❀ .... 👄 .... 💘 ....

Fav `social networking` site

✌ .... ❀ .... 👄 .... 💘 ....

Store in the mall you would NEVER SHOP IN

✌ .... ❀ .... 👄 .... 💘 ....

What makes you **superstitious**?

✌ .... ❀ .... 👄 .... 💘 ....

Fav music to dance to

✌ .... ❀ .... 👄 .... 💘 ....

Diet Coke, Coke, or Coke Zero?

✌ .... ❀ .... 👄 .... 💘 ....

Your bedroom: A total mess, Pretty neat, or So clean?

✌ .... ❀ .... 👄 .... 💘 ....

Better date idea: Picnic in the park, Ice cream and a movie, or Rollerblading?

✌ .... ❀ .... 👄 .... 💘 ....

Rate your **shopping habits** on a scale of **1** to **10**

✌ .... ❀ .... 👄 .... 💘 ....

Valentine's Day or HALLOWEEN?

✌ .... ✿ .... 👄 .... 💘 ....

Worst thing about being a girl

✌ .... ✿ .... 👄 .... 💘 ....

Best thing about being a girl

✌ .... ✿ .... 👄 .... 💘 ....

What you wear to the **beach**

✌ .... ✿ .... 👄 .... 💘 ....

Best **celeb body**

✌ .... ✿ .... 👄 .... 💘 ....

Who would **play you in a movie** of your life?

✌ .... ✿ .... 👄 .... 💘 ....

Have you ever been in *love*?

✌ .... ✿ .... 👄 .... 💘 ....

With who?

✌ .... ✿ .... 👄 .... 💘 ....

Best topping on a **sundae**?

✌ .... ✿ .... 👄 .... 💘 ....

You're a superhero: What's your special power?

✌ .... ✿ ....

👄 .... 💘 ....

Going to a dance: Limo with your girlfriends or solo dinner with your date?

✌ .... ❀ .... 👄 .... ♡ ....

Two things you *try and avoid*

✌ .... ❀ .... 👄 .... ♡ ....

Mini-dresses or **maxi dresses**?

✌ .... ❀ .... 👄 .... ♡ ....

Food that GROSSES you out

✌ .... ❀ .... 👄 .... ♡ ....

Horoscopes: Amazingly right or Such a joke?

✌ .... ❀ .... 👄 .... ♡ ....

You get to live **another country for a year**: Where do you go?

✌ .... ❀ .... 👄 .... ♡ ....

Sunbathing or skiing?

✌ .... ❀ .... 👄 .... ♡ ....

How long do you **talk** on the **phone** at **NIGHT**?

✌ .... ❀ .... 👄 .... ♡ ....

Fav brand of *lipgloss*

✌ .... ❀ .... 👄 .... ♡ ....

One thing in your **locker**

✌ .... ❀ .... 👄 .... ♡ ....

Fav color of **nail polish**

✌ .... ❀ .... 👄 .... 💘 ....

Babysitting: Worst job ever or Good gig?

✌ .... ❀ .... 👄 .... 💘 ....

Going out with a YOUNGER GUY: For sure or No way?

✌ .... ❀ .... 👄 .... 💘 ....

Stars or **hearts**?

✌ .... ❀ .... 👄 .... 💘 ....

Guy that *eats with his mouth open* or *wears dirty socks?*

✌ .... ❀ .... 👄 .... 💘 ....

New Year's Eve: So much fun! or Overrated?

✌ .... ❀ .... 👄 .... 💘 ....

Which **Monopoly** piece is your favorite?

✌ .... ❀ .... 👄 .... 💘 ....

Eat meatloaf every day for a week or **sing in front of the lunch room?**

✌ .... ❀ .... 👄 .... 💘 ....

What do you do when you *can't sleep?*

✌ .... ❀ .... 👄 .... 💘 ....

What's your **sign**?

✌ .... ❀ .... 👄 .... 💘 ....

Quiz:

What Kind of Friend Are You?

1. The guy your friend has a crush on called and asked you to a school dance. You:

a. Tell him you already have a date, even though you don't. (2 points)

b. Call her and ask her honest thoughts. Maybe you can all go together, as friends. (1 points)

c. Totally accept — why should you pass up a chance with one of the hottest guys in school? (3 points)

✌.......................... ❀.......................... 👄.......................... 💘..........................

2. One of your best girls wants you to help her egg another girl's house who she doesn't like. What do you do?

a. Plan your "It was her idea …" speech for if you get caught. (3 points)

b. Agree to go with her, even though you have nothing against the other girl. (2 points)

c. Suggest the girls talk about their issues and offer to play referee. (1 point)

✌.......................... ❀.......................... 👄.......................... 💘..........................

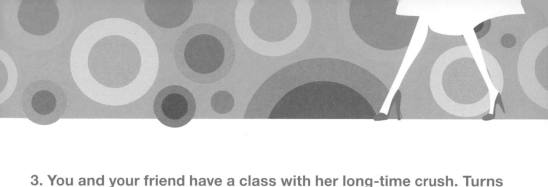

3. **You and your friend have a class with her long-time crush. Turns out he is really funny, so you:**

a. Encourage her to take the plunge and ask him to hang out! (1 point)
b. Laugh and giggle at his jokes. A little innocent flirting won't hurt anyone … (3 points)
c. Avoid him. You don't want her to get mad if she sees you talking to him. (2 points)

4. **You've started hanging out with some really popular girls who think your other friends are complete dorks. An old friend walks by while you are eating lunch with the popular girls. You:**

a. Say hi and introduce her to the other girls. (1 point)
b. Wave. (2 points)
c. Don't say anything. You'll catch up with her later when you're not busy. (3 points)

5. **Your friend never does her science homework, and she always asks to copy your answers. You:**

a. Turn her in for cheating. Why should she get credit for your work? (3 points)
b. Hand over your homework. (2 points)
c. Tell her you'll help her if she wants. (1 point)

6. A friend's boyfriend is notorious for having a wandering eye. Sure enough, when you run into him at a party, he tries to make a move on you. Your reaction?

a. "Back off creep. I'd never do that to my friend." (1 point)

b. Play along with it. You don't mind the attention, as long as she doesn't find out. (3 points)

c. Feel totally awkward, but don't say a word to her. (2 points)

✌ .... ❀ .... 👄 .... 💘 ....

7. You have plans to hang out with a friend, but then your crush miraculously calls and wants to have a study date. You:

a. Meet up with your friend and text message your crush the whole time. (2 points)

b. Call your friend and tell her you are going to have to bail on your plans. (3 points)

c. Curse the bad timing, but ask him for a rain-check. (1 point)

✌ .... ❀ .... 👄 .... 💘 ....

8. During a shopping trip, you and your best girl fall in love with the same red satin heels. Unfortunately, it's the last pair. You:

a. Tell her she can have them. (2 points)

b. Decide to split the cost and trade off who gets to wear them. They're that fabulous! (1 point)

c. Grab them. You saw them first! (3 points)

✌ .... ❀ .... 👄 .... 💘 ....

9. Your friend asks to borrow your favorite dress for a dance. What do you say?

a. Offer to lend her the shoes and purse that look good with it, too. (2 points)
b. Ask her if you can borrow something of hers and make a trade. (1 point)
c. Pretend it's at the cleaners — no one can look cuter than you in that dress. (3 points)

✌ .... ❀ .... 👄 .... 💘 ....

10. You made the volleyball team and your friend didn't. She's acting hurt and seems to be avoiding you. Your reaction?

a. Whatever, she's obviously jealous. (3 points)
b. Talk to her — assure her that this won't change your relationship. (1 point)
c. Tell her you won't join the team if it's going to hurt your friendship. (2 points)

✌ .... ❀ .... 👄 .... 💘 ....

11. Your friend asks for your help at her charity car wash on Saturday afternoon. You:

a. Totally help out and even make a few signs. (1 point)
b. Pretend you're busy. Why would you want to wash cars in your free time? (3 points)
c. Cancel the plans you already had made with your cousin. (2 points)

✌ .... ❀ .... 👄 .... 💘 ....

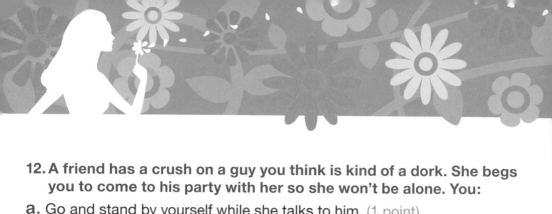

12. A friend has a crush on a guy you think is kind of a dork. She begs you to come to his party with her so she won't be alone. You:

a. Go and stand by yourself while she talks to him. (1 point)

b. Go and chat up his buddies. They're actually pretty cute, in that Michael Cera kind of way. (2 points)

c. Advise her that being seen at a nerd party is social suicide. (3 points)

✌ .... ❀ .... 👄 .... 💘 ....

12 to 20 points:

Best Friend: Congrats, you're a great friend! You recognize that unselfishness, honesty, and compromise make for best friends, and you don't let things like guys, grades, and popularity interfere with the girls you care about. Your friends know you always have their back, so they'll always have yours!

21 to 28 points:

Pushover Friend: You are thoughtful and often go out of your way to help your friends. However, you can be a bit of a doormat at times. Being a good friend doesn't mean dropping everything; it's more about having a good balance between being supportive and still an individual. Plus, it will make you and your girls closer if you stick up for yourself!

29 to 36 points:

Self-Involved Friend: How can you form great friendships if you're always looking out for yourself? Friendships shouldn't be competitive or one-sided. You don't want to be the kind of girl your friends think might flirt with their boyfriends or ditch them for someone "cooler," do you? Try to put your friends' feelings and needs first sometimes, and you will make friends for life.

Rate **sleeping in** on a scale of **1** to **10**

✌ .... ✿ .... 👄 .... 💘 ....

Would you rather win a **designer purse** or a trip to **Paris?**

✌ .... ✿ .... 👄 .... 💘 ....

Last *person* you *dreamt about*

✌ .... ✿ .... 👄 .... 💘 ....

Best **music** for when you're **feeling sad**

✌ .... ✿ .... 👄 .... 💘 ....

You can have **any name** other than your own: What do you choose?

✌ .... ✿ .... 👄 .... 💘 ....

Freckles: Pretty or Cover with makeup?

✌ .... ✿ .... 👄 .... 💘 ....

Roses or tulips?

✌ .... ✿ .... 👄 .... 💘 ....

Fav way to wear your *hair*

✌ .... ✿ .... 👄 .... 💘 ....

Unexpected guy you have a **crush** on

✌ .... ✿ .... 👄 .... 💘 ....

Dream job

✌ .... ✿ .... 👄 .... 💘 ....

FAV AGE to be

✌ .... ✿ .... 👄 .... ♡ ....

SCARIER: Spiders or bees?

✌ .... ✿ .... 👄 .... ♡ ....

Best new friend you met this year

✌ .... ✿ .... 👄 .... ♡ ....

How long does it take you to get ready for school?

✌ .... ✿ .... 👄 .... ♡ ....

Can you do a cartwheel?

✌ .... ✿ .... 👄 .... ♡ ....

One thing you're allergic to

✌ .... ✿ .... 👄 .... ♡ ....

Ever have a SUMMER CRUSH?

✌ .... ✿ .... 👄 .... ♡ ....

S'mores or hotdogs at a campfire?

✌ .... ✿ .... 👄 .... ♡ ....

Last thing you ate

✌ .... ✿ .... 👄 .... ♡ ....

Celeb you would approach for an autograph

✌ .... ✿ .... 👄 .... ♡ ....

Sunscreen: Never wear it, To the beach, or Every day?

✌ .... ❀ .... 👄 .... 💘 ....

Give up your cell phone or Sleep on the floor?

✌ .... ❀ .... 👄 .... 💘 ....

Fav **accessory**

✌ .... ❀ .... 👄 .... 💘 ....

Secondhand clothing stores: **Gold mine** or Ew, gross?

✌ .... ❀ .... 👄 .... 💘 ....

Rate your **cooking skills** on a scale of **1** to **10**

✌ .... ❀ .... 👄 .... 💘 ....

Ever dye **Easter** eggs?

✌ .... ❀ .... 👄 .... 💘 ....

Your **BIGGEST** indulgence

✌ .... ❀ .... 👄 .... 💘 ....

Last PERSON who MADE YOU CRY

✌ .... ❀ .... 👄 .... 💘 ....

WHAT DID HE OR SHE DO?

✌ .... ❀ .... 👄 .... 💘 ....

Fav Girl Scout **cookie**

✌ .... ❀ .... 👄 .... 💘 ....

What's worse: Black licorice or popcorn Jelly Bellies?

✌ .... 🌼 .... 👄 .... 💘 ....

Marilyn Monroe or *Audrey Hepburn*?

✌ .... 🌼 .... 👄 .... 💘 ....

Kiss on the **hand** or *Kiss* on the **forehead**?

✌ .... 🌼 .... 👄 .... 💘 ....

Bunny slippers or *ruffly nightgowns*?

✌ .... 🌼 .... 👄 .... 💘 ....

Guys in suits or **guys in sweats**?

✌ .... 🌼 .... 👄 .... 💘 ....

Fav **color** to wear

✌ .... 🌼 .... 👄 .... 💘 ....

Ever have *braces*?

✌ .... 🌼 .... 👄 .... 💘 ....

CLASS CLOWNS: Love em or Leave em?

✌ .... 🌼 .... 👄 .... 💘 ....

Best **book** for the **beach**

✌ .... 🌼 .... 👄 .... 💘 ....

Live at the **aquarium** or the **zoo**?

✌ .... 🌼 ....

👄 .... 💘 ....

Limo or a horse-drawn carriage?

✌ .... ❀ .... 👄 .... 💘 ....

Fav brand of *shampoo*

✌ .... ❀ .... 👄 .... 💘 ....

One thing in your **purse** right now

✌ .... ❀ .... 👄 .... 💘 ....

What's **under** your **bed**?

✌ .... ❀ .... 👄 .... 💘 ....

Ever *cry* in *class*?

✌ .... ❀ .... 👄 .... 💘 ....

Why?

✌ .... ❀ .... 👄 .... 💘 ....

More romantic: *The stars* or *the rain*?

✌ .... ❀ .... 👄 .... 💘 ....

Fav dish at **Thanksgiving** dinner

✌ .... ❀ .... 👄 .... 💘 ....

Meet the PRESIDENT or meet a `movie star`?

✌ .... ❀ .... 👄 .... 💘 ....

Fav thing that starts with C

✌ .... ❀ .... 👄 .... 💘 ....

Your **lucky** number

✌ .... ✿ .... 👄 .... 💘 ....

Ever been *teased*?

✌ .... ✿ .... 👄 .... 💘 ....

What about?

✌ .... ✿ .... 👄 .... 💘 ....

Ever liked a **guy who didn't like you** back?

✌ .... ✿ .... 👄 .... 💘 ....

The perfect *bra size* would be …

✌ .... ✿ .... 👄 .... 💘 ....

Colorblind or have **no sense of** **smell**?

✌ .... ✿ .... 👄 .... 💘 ....

Your **biggest** pet peeve

✌ .... ✿ .... 👄 .... 💘 ....

Ever play a *musical instrument*?

✌ .... ✿ .... 👄 .... 💘 ....

Best **dressed** celeb

✌ .... ✿ .... 👄 .... 💘 ....

Friend you'd move in with if your parents got abducted by aliens

✌ .... ✿ .... 👄 .... 💘 ....

What does the smell of the **ocean** remind you of?

✌ .... ❀ .... 👄 .... 💘 ....

You are planning your school's next dance: What theme do you choose?

✌ .... ❀ .... 👄 .... 💘 ....

Relationship status right now?

✌ .... ❀ .... 👄 .... 💘 ....

Love or lust?

✌ .... ❀ .... 👄 .... 💘 ....

Class you **wish** they **offered** at your **school**

✌ .... ❀ .... 👄 .... 💘 ....

Ever *shaved* your legs?

✌ .... ❀ .... 👄 .... 💘 ....

Who did you have your last **sleepover** with?

✌ .... ❀ .... 👄 .... 💘 ....

Ever **burped** in front of your crush?

✌ .... ❀ .... 👄 .... 💘 ....

Salt or **pepper**?

✌ .... ❀ .... 👄 .... 💘 ....

When do you think the **world** will **end**?

✌ .... ❀ .... 👄 .... 💘 ....

Cutest celeb couple

✌ .... ❀ .... 👄 .... 💘 ....

Can you tie a *cherry stem* in a knot with your *tongue*?

✌ .... ❀ .... 👄 .... 💘 ....

Ever been BURIED in the sand?

✌ .... ❀ .... 👄 .... 💘 ....

Can you **hula hoop**?

✌ .... ❀ .... 👄 .... 💘 ....

Walk up to your crush and *kiss* him or eat dog food?

✌ .... ❀ .... 👄 .... 💘 ....

Ever **hitchhiked**?

✌ .... ❀ .... 👄 .... 💘 ....

Best **Easter** candy

✌ .... ❀ .... 👄 .... 💘 ....

Kiss on the first date: If there's chemistry or Kinda sleazy?

✌ .... ❀ .... 👄 .... 💘 ....

It's your **16th** birthday and your parents get you a car with a big **red bow:** What kind is it?

✌ .... ❀ .... 👄 .... 💘 ....

Do you still sleep with a *stuffed animal*?

✌ .... ❀ .... 👄 .... 💘 ....

FAIL a **MATH** test or **FART** in front of your **FRIENDS**?

✌ .... ✿ .... 👄 .... 💘 ....

What do you normally EAT FOR BREAKFAST?

✌ .... ✿ .... 👄 .... 💘 ....

Tanning beds: **Golden tan** or **Bad for your health**?

✌ .... ✿ .... 👄 .... 💘 ....

Ever put **toothpaste** on a **zit**?

✌ .... ✿ .... 👄 .... 💘 ....

Bite your nails or addicted to the Internet?

✌ .... ✿ .... 👄 .... 💘 ....

Ever **stuff** your **bra**?

✌ .... ✿ .... 👄 .... 💘 ....

What's worse: Frizz or Split ends?

✌ .... ✿ .... 👄 .... 💘 ....

Something you do right **before bed**

✌ .... ✿ .... 👄 .... 💘 ....

Rate your last *kiss* on a scale of *1* to *10*

✌ .... ✿ .... 👄 .... 💘 ....

Best thing to do with **grandparents**

✌ .... ✿ .... 👄 .... 💘 ....

One thing you do to help the **environment**

Who would you cast a love spell on?

What **extreme sport** would you want to try?

Harry Potter or Twilight?

What do you like to wear that your parents don't approve of?

Fairy godmother or genie in a bottle?

Sport you are best at

What FORTUNE would you like to find in your FORTUNE COOKIE?

One word to describe the **last book you read**

Lake or RIVER?

Quiz:

What's Your Signature Scent?

1. Your friends would describe you as:
a. Girlie
b. Sassy and confident
c. Bubbly and friendly
d. Free-spirited
e. Sporty

2. On the weekends, you can be found:
a. On a romantic date with your crush
b. Dancing all night
c. Playing Frisbee with your friends
d. Writing a poem or song lyrics
e. Hanging out with your team

3. The flowers you'd like to get would be:
a. Roses
b. Orchids
c. Orange blossoms
d. You're not really into flowers — you'd prefer a cactus or cool plant
e. Violets

4. You would rather be (blank) than anywhere else.
a. Getting a pedicure
b. At a party
c. At the beach
d. Hiking in the mountains
e. Playing sports

✌ .... ❀ .... 👄 .... 💘 ....

5. When you hear your crush likes you, you:
a. Fall head over heels
b. Wear a flirty outfit to get him to notice you
c. Act really playful. You're optimistic he'll ask you out.
d. Play him a song you wrote on your guitar
e. Invite him to come watch your soccer game

✌ .... ❀ .... 👄 .... 💘 ....

6. When it comes to makeup, you:
a. Love it all — lipgloss, eyeshadow, blush, everything!
b. Like bold colors like deep purples and greens
c. Love lipgloss that tastes fruity
d. Wear earth tones like golds and browns
e. Don't wear much. You usually prefer a natural face.

✌ .... ❀ .... 👄 .... 💘 ....

7. An outfit you'd wear to school might be:
a. A cute dress and heels
b. Anything that turns heads
c. Your cheerleading uniform
d. A sundress and flip-flops
e. Jeans and a T-shirt

✌ .... ❀ .... 👄 .... 💘 ....

8. During the summer, you like to:
a. Go bikini shopping
b. Throw a fabulous pool party
c. Go to an amusement park or water park
d. Watch the sunset with your crush
e. Spend a day at the beach — maybe play volleyball

9. During the winter, you like to:
a. Snuggle up with hot cocoa and a cute guy
b. Wear cashmere
c. Start a snowball fight
d. Stay inside and draw or paint
e. Find the best snow for snowboarding or skiing

10. Your favorite color is:
a. Pink
b. Black
c. Yellow
d. Green
e. Blue

Mostly a's:

Floral: You are a girlie girl who likes to look pretty and feminine. You also tend to be a hopeless romantic. Your signature scent is anything soft and romantic, with notes of rose, gardenia, jasmine, or lavender.

Mostly b's:

Oriental: You are confident and passionate and never shy away from attention. You dress to be noticed and want an exotic scent that's perfect for dancing all night long. Try spicy scents that include vanilla, clove, orchid, or cinnamon in their notes.

Mostly c's:

Fruity/Citrus: You are fun and playful, with a carefree attitude. You're almost always happy and cheerful and need a light-hearted scent. Your signature scent should have juicy notes of orange, grapefruit, apple, or lemon.

Mostly d's:

Woody: You're a creative girl with a free spirit. You are an artist, poet, singer, or writer who loves to be out in nature. The perfect scent for you will incorporate sandalwood, amber, cedar, moss, or even leather.

Mostly e's:

Fresh: You are sporty and tend to stay away from anything super girlie. You prefer a natural, clean look that lets your confident personality show through. Choose a perfume with clean water-based notes, such as rain, grass, freesia, or lotus flower.

Hairy feet or *shave your eyebrows*?

✌ .... ❀ .... 👄 .... 💘 ....

Weirdest movie you've seen

✌ .... ❀ .... 👄 .... 💘 ....

Last thing you **complimented** someone on

✌ .... ❀ .... 👄 .... 💘 ....

What's worse: Broken heart or a broken arm?

✌ .... ❀ .... 👄 .... 💘 ....

Keeping a diary: Dumb or Cathartic?

✌ .... ❀ .... 👄 .... 💘 ....

Rate your most **embarrassing moment** on a scale of **1** to **10**

✌ .... ❀ .... 👄 .... 💘 ....

Purse dogs or **big dogs**?

✌ .... ❀ .... 👄 .... 💘 ....

Most meaningful piece of **jewelry**

✌ .... ❀ .... 👄 .... 💘 ....

Who gave it to you?

✌ .... ❀ .... 👄 .... 💘 ....

Long hair on guys: **Hot** or **Not**?

✌ .... ❀ .... 👄 .... 💘 ....

Ever read a *romance novel*?

✌ .... ✿ .... 👄 .... 💘 ....

Where would you want to get **married**?

✌ .... ✿ .... 👄 .... 💘 ....

Do you have a credit card?

✌ .... ✿ .... 👄 .... 💘 ....

Would you ever be a **vegetarian**?

✌ .... ✿ .... 👄 .... 💘 ....

Lemons or limes?

✌ .... ✿ .... 👄 .... 💘 ....

Ever won a **contest**?

✌ .... ✿ .... 👄 .... 💘 ....

Fav *hair* product

✌ .... ✿ .... 👄 .... 💘 ....

Awards show you'd most like to attend

✌ .... ✿ .... 👄 .... 💘 ....

Fav Olympic sport

✌ .... ✿ .... 👄 .... 💘 ....

Date a guy with a **wooden leg** or an **eye patch**?

✌ .... ✿ ....

👄 .... 💘 ....

Prettiest language to speak

✌ .... ✿ .... 👄 .... ♡ ....

Most POINTLESS part of your school day

✌ .... ✿ .... 👄 .... ♡ ....

In **3 years**, you will be ….

✌ .... ✿ .... 👄 .... ♡ ....

Spiders: Squash 'em or Save 'em?

✌ .... ✿ .... 👄 .... ♡ ....

Worse pain: Paper cut or stubbed toe?

✌ .... ✿ .... 👄 .... ♡ ....

What FICTIONAL CHARACTER do you wish was real?

✌ .... ✿ .... 👄 .... ♡ ....

Ever met anyone famous?

✌ .... ✿ .... 👄 .... ♡ ....

You are **hopeless** at …

✌ .... ✿ .... 👄 .... ♡ ....

Best farm animal

✌ .... ✿ .... 👄 .... ♡ ....

Ever dot your **i's** with a *heart*?

✌ .... ✿ .... 👄 .... ♡ ....

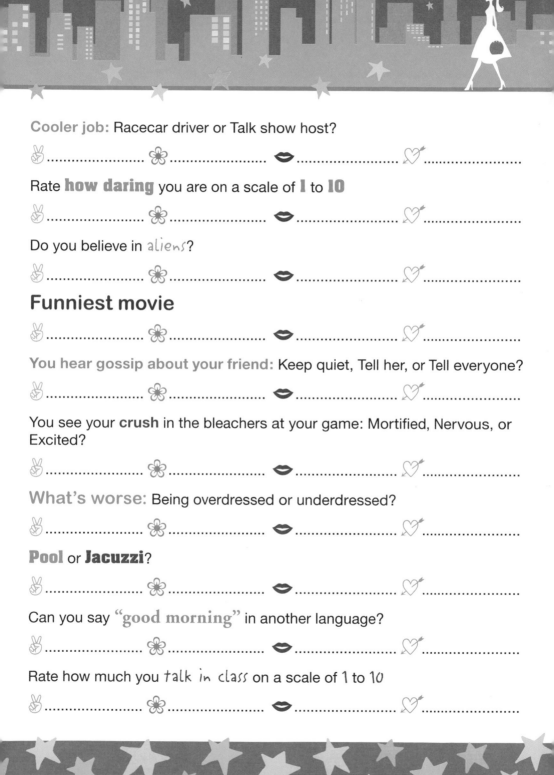

Cooler job: Racecar driver or Talk show host?

✌ .... 🌼 .... 👄 .... 💘 ....

Rate **how daring** you are on a scale of **1** to **10**

✌ .... 🌼 .... 👄 .... 💘 ....

Do you believe in aliens?

✌ .... 🌼 .... 👄 .... 💘 ....

Funniest movie

✌ .... 🌼 .... 👄 .... 💘 ....

You hear gossip about your friend: Keep quiet, Tell her, or Tell everyone?

✌ .... 🌼 .... 👄 .... 💘 ....

You see your **crush** in the bleachers at your game: Mortified, Nervous, or Excited?

✌ .... 🌼 .... 👄 .... 💘 ....

What's worse: Being overdressed or underdressed?

✌ .... 🌼 .... 👄 .... 💘 ....

Pool or **Jacuzzi**?

✌ .... 🌼 .... 👄 .... 💘 ....

Can you say "good morning" in another language?

✌ .... 🌼 .... 👄 .... 💘 ....

Rate how much you talk in class on a scale of 1 to 10

✌ .... 🌼 .... 👄 .... 💘 ....

Ever ride a Ferris wheel?

Coffee or tea?

Fav thing to do on a **rainy day**

Best way to waste an hour

Ever **movie-hop**?

You're a world-class athlete: Which sport do you choose?

Fav way to de-stress

Ponytail or **pigtails**?

Passing notes in class: **Fun** or **immature**?

Ever lie to someone in this room to protect her **feelings**?

What **about?**

✌ .... ✿ .... 👄 .... 💘 ....

Count calories or eat what you want?

✌ .... ✿ .... 👄 .... 💘 ....

Ride the **bus to school** or have your **mom drive you**?

✌ .... ✿ .... 👄 .... 💘 ....

Rate how badly you **procrastinate** on a scale of **1** to **10**

✌ .... ✿ .... 👄 .... 💘 ....

McDonald's or **Burger King**?

✌ .... ✿ .... 👄 .... 💘 ....

You like your guy friend as more than a friend: Tell him or Mouth shut?

✌ .... ✿ .... 👄 .... 💘 ....

Flats or heels?

✌ .... ✿ .... 👄 .... 💘 ....

COUNTRY CHICK or **city chick**?

✌ .... ✿ .... 👄 .... 💘 ....

Are you a guy's girl or a girlie girl?

✌ .... ✿ .... 👄 .... 💘 ....

Sugar or **Splenda**?

✌ .... ✿ .... 👄 .... 💘 ....

TYPE IN ALL CAPS or all lowercase?

✌ .... ❀ .... 👄 .... 💘 ....

Got any *hidden talents*?

✌ .... ❀ .... 👄 .... 💘 ....

What's your **middle name**?

✌ .... ❀ .... 👄 .... 💘 ....

You find a wallet with $100: Return it or Keep the money?

✌ .... ❀ .... 👄 .... 💘 ....

Last thing you and your best friend *fought over*

✌ .... ❀ .... 👄 .... 💘 ....

One thing you're **wearing today**

✌ .... ❀ .... 👄 .... 💘 ....

How many days a week do you **work out**?

✌ .... ❀ .... 👄 .... 💘 ....

VAMPIRES or **WEREWOLVES**?

✌ .... ❀ .... 👄 .... 💘 ....

One thing that makes you feel **anxious**

✌ .... ❀ .... 👄 .... 💘 ....

Last thing you were *complimented* on

✌ .... ❀ .... 👄 .... 💘 ....

Open-minded or opinionated?

✌ .... ✿ .... 👄 .... 💘 ....

Ever eat **Mexican food** at 2 a.m.?

✌ .... ✿ .... 👄 .... 💘 ....

One person who you would never invite to a *party*

✌ .... ✿ .... 👄 .... 💘 ....

Last thing that **SCARED** you

✌ .... ✿ .... 👄 .... 💘 ....

Your most **trusted** friend is …

✌ .... ✿ .... 👄 .... 💘 ....

A **guy friend** people always say you should date

✌ .... ✿ .... 👄 .... 💘 ....

Moody or **even-tempered**?

✌ .... ✿ .... 👄 .... 💘 ....

One **reality TV** show you would like to be on

✌ .... ✿ .... 👄 .... 💘 ....

Funniest actor

✌ .... ✿ .... 👄 .... 💘 ....

One thing your typical **school day** includes

✌ .... ✿ .... 👄 .... 💘 ....

Worst song on the radio

✌ .... ❀ .... 👄 .... ♡ ....

People who **talk too much** make you feel …

✌ .... ❀ .... 👄 .... ♡ ....

Coolest sporting event you've attended

✌ .... ❀ .... 👄 .... ♡ ....

Fav **CITY** you've visited

✌ .... ❀ .... 👄 .... ♡ ....

Would you rather visit the Eiffel Tower, Times Square, or the Egyptian pyramids?

✌ .... ❀ .... 👄 .... ♡ ....

You're stuck on a DESERT ISLAND: What one thing do you bring with you?

✌ .... ❀ .... 👄 .... ♡ ....

Ever kept a piece of an **ex's clothing**?

✌ .... ❀ .... 👄 .... ♡ ....

What was it?

✌ .... ❀ .... 👄 .... ♡ ....

Rate **sushi** on a scale of **1** to **10**

✌ .... ❀ .... 👄 .... ♡ ....

Wear a *tutu* or *leotard*?

✌ .... ❀ .... 👄 .... ♡ ....

Ever have an **imaginary** friend?

✌ .... ❀ .... 👄 .... ♡ ....

What was his or her *name*?

✌ .... ❀ .... 👄 .... ♡ ....

Ever *kissed* more than one person in one week?

✌ .... ❀ .... 👄 .... ♡ ....

What's your **best bowling score**?

✌ .... ❀ .... 👄 .... ♡ ....

Swimming or *sunning*?

✌ .... ❀ .... 👄 .... ♡ ....

Ever had a **CRUSH** on a neighbor?

✌ .... ❀ .... 👄 .... ♡ ....

Who?

✌ .... ❀ .... 👄 .... ♡ ....

One thing in your **dream house**

✌ .... ❀ .... 👄 .... ♡ ....

More fun: Being single or being part of a couple?

✌ .... ❀ .... 👄 .... ♡ ....

One thing you would **CHaNGe** about guys

✌ .... ❀ .... 👄 .... ♡ ....

Quiz:

How Superficial are You?

1. Your favorite thing about your crush is:

a. Every girl in your grade wishes she could date him. *(1 point)*

b. He's freakin' hot. What else is there? *(2 points)*

c. He makes you laugh (and he's pretty cute, too). *(3 points)*

 ....

2. Your friend wants to set you up on a blind date. The first thing you want to know about the guy is:

a. His name. *(3 points)*

b. What kind of car he drives. *(2 points)*

c. How tall he is and what color eyes he has. *(1 point)*

....

3. You show up at your best friend's house and you are both accidentally wearing the same dress! You:

a. Roll your eyes, but really, you look better in it anyway. *(1 point)*

b. Make her go back inside and change. *(2 points)*

c. Joke with everyone that you planned it. *(3 points)*

....

4. Your crush picks you up for the dance in his brother's old car. You:

a. Fume all night. How embarrassing to be pulling up to school like this. *(2 points)*

b. Are so happy to be going with him! *(3 points)*

c. Secretly wish you were taking a limo instead. *(1 point)*

5. You are supposed to go to a friend's birthday party — plus, your crush is invited. But you wake up with a huge zit right on your nose. You:

a. Dab cover-up on it and forget about it. If you don't bring attention to it, no one else will notice. *(3 points)*

b. Cover it with makeup and check it in the mirror every 30 minutes throughout the party. *(1 point)*

c. Stay home, there's no way anyone can see you like this. *(2 points)*

....

6. Your parents refuse to pay $300 for a prom dress. You:

a. Save every dollar you make babysitting until you can buy the best dress. *(1 point)*

b. Throw a temper tantrum. You can't be seen in anything less. *(2 points)*

c. Find a cute dress at a vintage store. You'll be the only one wearing it! *(3 points)*

7. Shopping at secondhand stores is:

a. Out of the question. You only wear certain brands, sorry. *(2 points)*

b. Fine, as long as no one knows. *(1 point)*

c. A great way to save money and find cute clothes. *(3 points)*

✌ .... ❀ .... 👄 .... 💘 ....

8. Your best friend starts dating a new guy. When you meet him for the first time, you think:

a. "He seems to really like her!" *(3 points)*

b. "Um, he must have a great personality." *(1 point)*

c. "He needs a wardrobe makeover. And a haircut. And contacts." *(2 points)*

✌ .... ❀ .... 👄 .... 💘 ....

9. How many times a day do you check yourself out in the mirror?

a. When you're washing your hands in the bathroom. *(3 points)*

b. For periodic makeup touchups throughout the day. *(1 point)*

c. Every time you walk by a window or shiny surface. *(2 points)*

✌ .... ❀ .... 👄 .... 💘 ....

10. You choose your friends based on:

a. How pretty and popular they are. *(2 points)*

b. How similar you all are. *(1 point)*

c. How much fun you have together. *(3 points)*

✌ .... ❀ .... 👄 .... 💘 ....

10 to 16 points:

One-Dimensional.

You care so much about what other people think that it's turned you into a one-dimensional robot! Fitting in and being liked aren't the most important things in life — and the more you stress about them, the harder it is to figure out who you truly are. Try taking a deeper look inside your friends and crushes, and yourself.

17 to 23 points:

So Shallow.

People find it hard to get to know and like you because it seems like all you care about are having nice clothes and dating a cute guy. If you start appreciating more than what's skin-deep you'll find you make better friends and have longer-lasting relationships. People will value you for more than the superficial.

24 to 30 points:

Genuine Girl.

You don't stress out too much about material things. You know that being real and unselfish will get you much further than being pretty and having a hot boyfriend. People trust you and want to be your friend because they know you'll see deeper than what's on the outside.

SUV or *sports car*?

✌ .... ✿ .... 👄 .... 💘 ....

Ever lent a friend **money $$$**?

✌ .... ✿ .... 👄 .... 💘 ....

COWBOY BOOTS or STILETTOS?

✌ .... ✿ .... 👄 .... 💘 ....

Ever had a **crush** on a teacher?

✌ .... ✿ .... 👄 .... 💘 ....

Which one?

✌ .... ✿ .... 👄 .... 💘 ....

(Blank) always makes you *laugh*

✌ .... ✿ .... 👄 .... 💘 ....

Bigger **deal-breaker** in a guy: Bad teeth or smoking?

✌ .... ✿ .... 👄 .... 💘 ....

Your WORST HABIT

✌ .... ✿ .... 👄 .... 💘 ....

Rate your *shoe collection* on a scale of *1* to *10*

✌ .... ✿ .... 👄 .... 💘 ....

Are you more **AFRAID** of needles or heights?

✌ .... ✿ .... 👄 .... 💘 ....

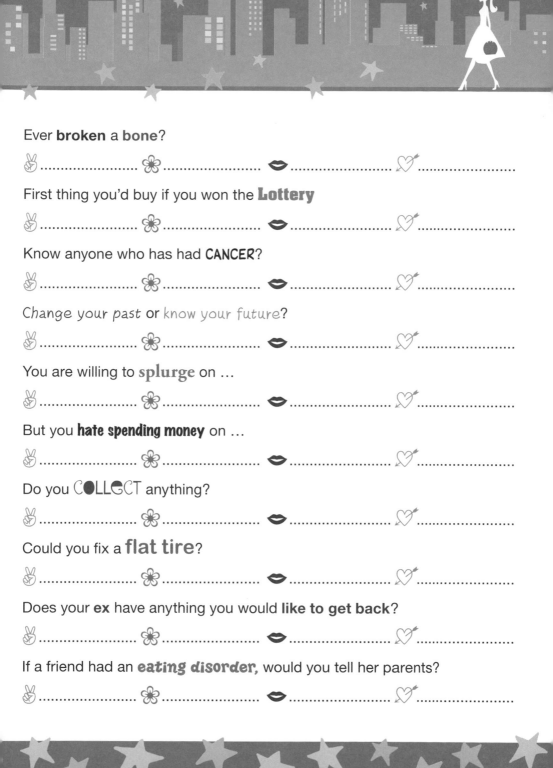

Ever **broken** a bone?

✌ .... ❀ .... 👄 .... ♡ ....

First thing you'd buy if you won the **Lottery**

✌ .... ❀ .... 👄 .... ♡ ....

Know anyone who has had **CANCER**?

✌ .... ❀ .... 👄 .... ♡ ....

Change your *past* or know your future?

✌ .... ❀ .... 👄 .... ♡ ....

You are willing to **splurge** on …

✌ .... ❀ .... 👄 .... ♡ ....

But you **hate spending money** on …

✌ .... ❀ .... 👄 .... ♡ ....

Do you C●LL●CT anything?

✌ .... ❀ .... 👄 .... ♡ ....

Could you fix a **flat tire**?

✌ .... ❀ .... 👄 .... ♡ ....

Does your **ex** have anything you would **like to get back**?

✌ .... ❀ .... 👄 .... ♡ ....

If a friend had an **eating disorder,** would you tell her parents?

✌ .... ❀ .... 👄 .... ♡ ....

Ever **flirted** to get something?

....

What was it?

....

Rate your **school picture** on a scale of **1** to **10**

....

What's **grosser**: Moldy fruit or spoiled milk?

....

Ever gotten **revenge** on someone? Who?

....

What did *that person do* to you?

....

Top QUALITY you need in a friend

....

Best **music** for getting ready for a **party**

....

Sour or *sweet candy*?

....

Rate how **good of a dancer** you are on a scale of **1** to **10**

....

What gives you GOOSEBUMPS?

✌ .... ✿ .... 👄 .... ♡ ....

Least favorite band?

✌ .... ✿ .... 👄 .... ♡ ....

Head massage or **foot massage**?

✌ .... ✿ .... 👄 .... ♡ ....

How many *pairs of shoes* do you own?

✌ .... ✿ .... 👄 .... ♡ ....

You wish your **worst enemy** would move to …

✌ .... ✿ .... 👄 .... ♡ ....

Top thing you're **grateful** for right now

✌ .... ✿ .... 👄 .... ♡ ....

Do you mind being *tickled*?

✌ .... ✿ .... 👄 .... ♡ ....

Coolest place you went in the last year

✌ .... ✿ .... 👄 .... ♡ ....

Recent event that really IMPACTED you

✌ .... ✿ .... 👄 .... ♡ ....

How happy are you with your body?

✌ .... ✿ .... 👄 .... ♡ ....

Quiz:

What's Your Travel Personality?

1. You're traveling to the rainforests of Costa Rica. Which activity sounds best to you?
a. Taking a zipline through the jungle
b. Doing a group yoga class and meeting new people
c. Taking a tour of the ancient ruins and viewing the wildlife
d. Napping on the beach

✌ .... ❀ .... 👄 .... ♡ ....

2. If you could choose, you would:
a. Take an action-packed trip complete with bungee-jumping, hiking, and scuba diving
b. Take a roadtrip with your best girlfriends
c. Backpack through Europe on your own and visit several different countries
d. Spend a week at a secluded spa

✌ .... ❀ .... 👄 .... ♡ ....

3. On vacation, you would never want to:
a. Lay by the pool all day
b. Travel alone
c. Travel with a big group of family or friends
d. Plan a lot of excursions

✌ .... ❀ .... 👄 .... ♡ ....

4. Which would you order when you're out to dinner?
a. A special kind of sushi you've never tried
b. A big cheese and fruit plate that everyone can share
c. The specialty of the house, at the chef's recommendation
d. The first thing that catches your eye — you like to make it easy

5. Where would you most like to stay on vacation?
a. An all-inclusive resort that offers daily activities
b. A fun trendy hotel with lots of young people
c. Whatever is closest to the museums, landmarks, and restaurants
d. A resort with an awesome pool and spa

6. Which one of these people would you like to meet?
a. World traveler
b. Manhattan socialite
c. World famous chef de cuisine
d. Indian yoga guru

....

7. You made $200 babysitting! What do you put it toward?
a. Skydiving
b. A day at an amusement park with all your girlfriends
c. Tickets for you and a date to an awesome Broadway show
d. Massage and facial

8. Parent-teacher conferences means no school! Where do you go?
a. Take a surfing lesson
b. Call a few friends and have a pool party
c. Go see a historical landmark in your city that you've never visited
d. Read, take a nap, paint your toes

✌ .... ❀ .... 👄 .... ♡ ....

9. What are you most likely to bring on a vacation?
a. Hiking boots
b. This journal!
c. A tour guide book
d. Noise-canceling headphones

✌ .... ❀ .... 👄 .... ♡ ....

10. If you were in Paris, you'd prefer to:
a. Eat frog's legs and snails — to say you have!
b. Go dancing and meet the locals
c. Sit at a café and soak up the environment
d. Go shopping

✌ .... ❀ .... 👄 .... ♡ ....

Mostly a's: Adventure Traveler: You like to use your travel time to do everything and anything out of the ordinary, whether it be an adventure sport, eating an exotic food, or trying all the activities a resort offers. You'll get along best with Culture Junkies and others of your kind. Try all-inclusive resorts that provide daily activities, or seek out trips that take you on outdoorsy adventures. Just be aware that your stacked itinerary may scare off Relaxation Seekers.

Mostly b's: **Bonding Babe:** Your favorite part of taking a vacation is spending quality time with your fellow travelers, best friends, and new people you meet. You're super social, so you prefer traveling in a pack, especially with your girls. You enjoy any activity that includes bonding time with your group or chatting up other vacationers. Try taking a cruise, staying at a resort with other families, or planning a mini-vacay for you and your friends.

Mostly c's: **Culture Junkie:** Lying by a pool seems like a waste of time to you! You like to soak up the culture of the city or country you're visiting. Your trip itinerary always includes museums, art galleries, plays, monuments, and other famous landmarks. You don't mind traveling alone, because it lets you make every stop on your list, but if you go with others, travel with Adventure Travelers or other Culture Junkies. Try visiting cities with history and culture around every corner, like Washington D.C., New York City, San Francisco, Paris, or Florence, Italy.

Mostly d's: **Relaxation Seeker:** When you travel, you're looking for rest and relaxation — there isn't much (or any) sightseeing on your itinerary. Beach trips and spa weekends are right up your alley, and you might also try planning a "staycation," where you create a vacation right at home! Shut off your cell phone and computer, grab a good book, and spend some time chilling out and recharging. You can travel with anyone, as long as they understand you'll be poolside while they're hitting the museum circuit.

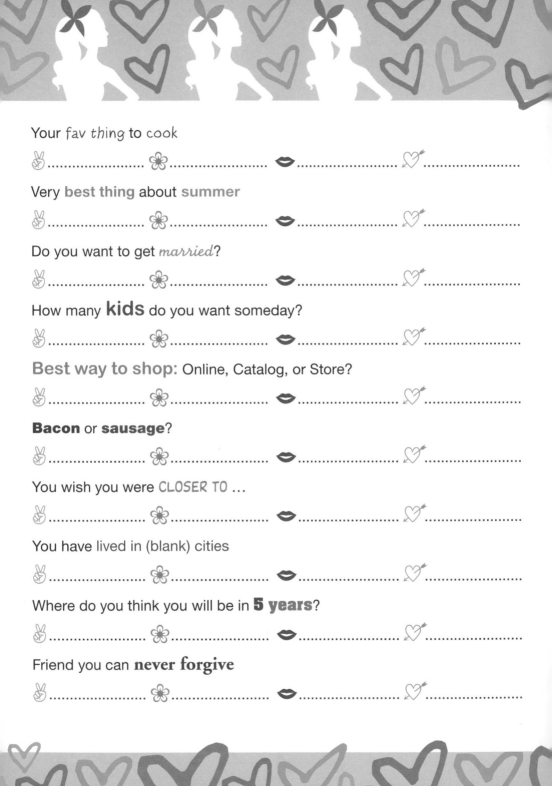

Your *fav thing* to cook

✌ .... ✿ .... 👄 .... ♡ ....

Very **best thing** about **summer**

✌ .... ✿ .... 👄 .... ♡ ....

Do you want to get *married*?

✌ .... ✿ .... 👄 .... ♡ ....

How many **kids** do you want someday?

✌ .... ✿ .... 👄 .... ♡ ....

Best way to shop: Online, Catalog, or Store?

✌ .... ✿ .... 👄 .... ♡ ....

Bacon or **sausage**?

✌ .... ✿ .... 👄 .... ♡ ....

You wish you were CLOSER TO …

✌ .... ✿ .... 👄 .... ♡ ....

You have lived in (blank) cities

✌ .... ✿ .... 👄 .... ♡ ....

Where do you think you will be in **5 years**?

✌ .... ✿ .... 👄 .... ♡ ....

Friend you can **never forgive**

✌ .... ✿ .... 👄 .... ♡ ....

Do you pinch people not wearing green on **St. Patrick's Day**?

✌ .... ✿ .... 👄 .... ♡ ....

Would you rather miss your plane or have the airline lose your luggage for a day?

✌ .... ✿ .... 👄 .... ♡ ....

Best **breakup** song

✌ .... ✿ .... 👄 .... ♡ ....

Would you **divorce your parents** if you could?

✌ .... ✿ .... 👄 .... ♡ ....

Last person you **hugged**?

✌ .... ✿ .... 👄 .... ♡ ....

Famous LANDMARK you would like to visit

✌ .... ✿ .... 👄 .... ♡ ....

Last *rollercoaster* you rode

✌ .... ✿ .... 👄 .... ♡ ....

Your most *sentimental* piece of clothing

✌ .... ✿ .... 👄 .... ♡ ....

Go on an **African safari** or ski the **Swiss Alps**?

✌ .... ✿ .... 👄 .... ♡ ....

Rate how competitive you are on a scale of 1 to 10

✌ .... ✿ .... 👄 .... ♡ ....

Shout or whisper?

✌ .... ❀ .... 👄 .... 💘 ....

Live in the **ocean** or be able to **fly**?

✌ .... ❀ .... 👄 .... 💘 ....

ENERGY DRINKS: Ick! or Tasty?

✌ .... ❀ .... 👄 .... 💘 ....

Ever turned in a *cheater*?

✌ .... ❀ .... 👄 .... 💘 ....

Swim with sharks or **tame lions?**

✌ .... ❀ .... 👄 .... 💘 ....

Wear your clothes inside out **or** *fail your English test?*

✌ .... ❀ .... 👄 .... 💘 ....

How much money would you have to get paid to eat a live bug?

✌ .... ❀ .... 👄 .... 💘 ....

EVER SHOT A GUN?

✌ .... ❀ .... 👄 .... 💘 ....

Would you rather be a *little hotter* or a *lot smarter*?

✌ .... ❀ .... 👄 .... 💘 ....

Read the **book** or see the **movie**?

✌ .... ❀ .... 👄 .... 💘 ....

Ever **crashed** a **party**?

✌ .... ✿ .... 👄 .... 💘 ....

WOULD YOU RATHER have the hiccups for a year or wear braces for 10 years?

✌ .... ✿ .... 👄 .... 💘 ....

What's the **WORST WAY** to **DIE**?

✌ .... ✿ .... 👄 .... 💘 ....

Live in an **igloo** or **cave**?

✌ .... ✿ .... 👄 .... 💘 ....

One thing you'd save in a FIRE

✌ .... ✿ .... 👄 .... 💘 ....

What kind of **dessert** would you be?

✌ .... ✿ .... 👄 .... 💘 ....

HALLOWEEN: Dress sexy or Dress scary?

✌ .... ✿ .... 👄 .... 💘 ....

Rate how *nervous you get for tests* on a scale of 1 to 10

✌ .... ✿ .... 👄 .... 💘 ....

Would you get **hair extensions**?

✌ .... ✿ .... 👄 .... 💘 ....

WHAT'S WORSE: Going to the doctor or the dentist?

✌ .... ✿ .... 👄 .... 💘 ....

Tire swings: **Awesome** or **Makes you dizzy?**

....

Sport you'd like to try

....

Would you rather meet the guy of your dreams or lose 20 pounds?

....

First CD

....

Do you *kiss and tell*?

....

Are you an OPTIMIST, **PESSIMIST**, or REALIST?

....

Fav **TV** couple

....

Rate your **pop culture** knowledge on a scale of **1** to **10**

....

Muffins or crossaints?

....

What teacher always **catches you talking** in class?

....

Best store for accessories

✌ .... ❀ .... 👄 .... 💘 ....

Rate how **artistic** you are on a scale of **1** to **10**

✌ .... ❀ .... 👄 .... 💘 ....

One friend who needs a *makeover*

✌ .... ❀ .... 👄 .... 💘 ....

Fav thing to do at a **sleepover** (aside from this book)

✌ .... ❀ .... 👄 .... 💘 ....

How many pieces of **pizza** do you usually eat?

✌ .... ❀ .... 👄 .... 💘 ....

Ever *cheated* on a test?

✌ .... ❀ .... 👄 .... 💘 ....

Fav **board game**

✌ .... ❀ .... 👄 .... 💘 ....

Do you take any **vitamins**?

✌ .... ❀ .... 👄 .... 💘 ....

Would you ever go out with your *friend's ex*?

✌ .... ❀ .... 👄 .... 💘 ....

Fav **junk** food

✌ .... ❀ .... 👄 .... 💘 ....

Quiz:

What's Your Guy Style?

1. **Your date picks you up for a dance. He arrives:**
a. With a dozen red roses, in a limo
b. Early so he can say hello to your parents
c. An hour late. But he holds the car door for you.

✌ .... ❀ .... 👄 .... ♡ ....

2. **When you mention your crush's name, your friends:**
a. Swoon
b. Say, "You mean the guy from your math class?"
c. All know at least one girl he's gone out with

✌ .... ❀ .... 👄 .... ♡ ....

3. **When he calls at night, he:**
a. Plays you a song on his guitar
b. He's kind of quiet, but makes you smile
c. Clicks over to the other line every 5 minutes to take another call

✌ .... ❀ .... 👄 .... ♡ ....

4. When you and your guy go to a party together, he:

a. Stays by your side the whole night, usually holding your hand

b. Knows every guy on the baseball team. Turns out he's the team tutor!

c. Disappears, and you find him chatting up a group of girls

 ....

5. The cutest thing your crush ever did was:

a. Write you a poem

b. Pick you a bouquet of wildflowers

c. Choose you over his other Friday night date options

....

6. Guys you avoid like the plague include:

a. Shy guys who can't express their feelings

b. Cocky jock types

c. Like they say, nice guys finish last

....

7. Your guy brings over a romantic movie for your date. He chooses:

a. *Romeo and Juliet*

b. *Can't Hardly Wait*

c. *Cruel Intentions*

....

....

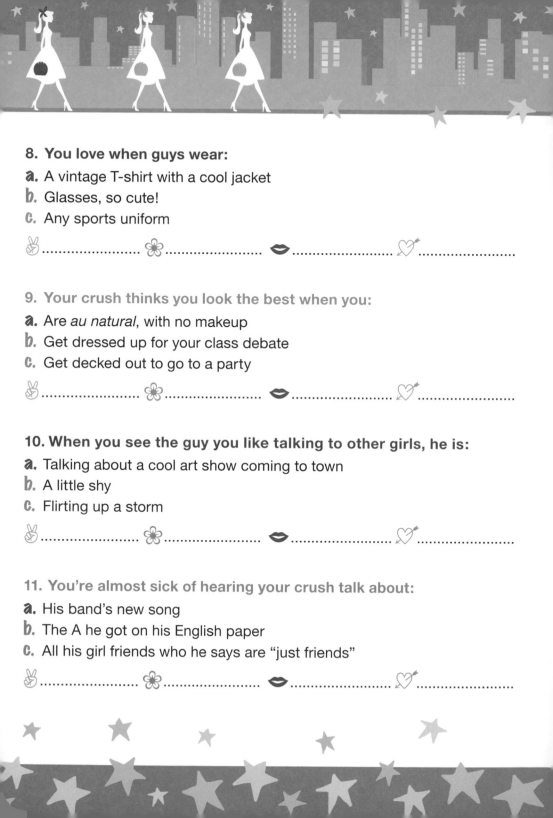

8. You love when guys wear:

a. A vintage T-shirt with a cool jacket

b. Glasses, so cute!

c. Any sports uniform

✌ .... ✿ .... 👄 .... 💘 ....

9. Your crush thinks you look the best when you:

a. Are *au natural*, with no makeup

b. Get dressed up for your class debate

c. Get decked out to go to a party

✌ .... ✿ .... 👄 .... 💘 ....

10. When you see the guy you like talking to other girls, he is:

a. Talking about a cool art show coming to town

b. A little shy

c. Flirting up a storm

✌ .... ✿ .... 👄 .... 💘 ....

11. You're almost sick of hearing your crush talk about:

a. His band's new song

b. The A he got on his English paper

c. All his girl friends who he says are "just friends"

✌ .... ✿ .... 👄 .... 💘 ....

12. Your parents think the guy you're dating:

a. Might run off to New York to become an actor
b. Will definitely get into a great college
c. Is hopefully a phase

★ Mostly a's: *Artsy Romantic*

You like a guy who can really express his feelings — and who better than an artist or musician? A creative guy who's in touch with his emotions is wonderful, just be careful he doesn't get too mushy or disappear for a month with his garage band.

★ Mostly b's: *Sweet Smarty*

You're definitely attracted to the smart, nice guys who get good grades and make friends easily. While some girls like a bad boy to keep a relationship exciting, you much prefer a cute borderline nerd — he'll always remember your birthday and charm you with his wide vocabulary.

★ Mostly c's: *Play-It-Cool Player*

Unfortunately, you're drawn to the player type. He might be a popular guy, jock, or bad boy, but he always means trouble. Because he's got girls nipping at his heels at all times, he doesn't feel the need to go out of his way for you. Ditch the "too cool" attitude for a guy who's a little more attentive.

What totally gives you a HEADACHE?

✌ .... ❀ .... 👄 .... 💘 ....

Ride your bike to **school**: No way!, Totally, or Too far?

✌ .... ❀ .... 👄 .... 💘 ....

Fav place to **study**

✌ .... ❀ .... 👄 .... 💘 ....

SCARY test you have coming up

✌ .... ❀ .... 👄 .... 💘 ....

Rate how **confident** you are on a scale of **1** to **10**

✌ .... ❀ .... 👄 .... 💘 ....

How tasty is a big *juicy steak*: Delicious or I'll pass?

✌ .... ❀ .... 👄 .... 💘 ....

Waking up **early** is (blank)

✌ .... ❀ .... 👄 .... 💘 ....

The NEXT TIME you'll see your MOM

✌ .... ❀ .... 👄 .... 💘 ....

Best store to **bra shop**

✌ .... ❀ .... 👄 .... 💘 ....

Last MOVIE you saw

✌ .... ❀ .... 👄 .... 💘 ....

Arcade games **or** rollercoasters?

✌ .... ❀ .... 👄 .... ♡ ....

Would you **blog** every day about **your life**?

✌ .... ❀ .... 👄 .... ♡ ....

What makes you *blush*?

✌ .... ❀ .... 👄 .... ♡ ....

Where did you go last **spring break**?

✌ .... ❀ .... 👄 .... ♡ ....

Your *ringtone* right now

✌ .... ❀ .... 👄 .... ♡ ....

Ever **invented** something?

✌ .... ❀ .... 👄 .... ♡ ....

Do your parents disapprove of the music you listen to?

✌ .... ❀ .... 👄 .... ♡ ....

Fav author

✌ .... ❀ .... 👄 .... ♡ ....

Do you believe in *love at first sight*?

✌ .... ❀ .... 👄 .... ♡ ....

Your ex-boy: *Kiss* **or** *diss*?

✌ .... ❀ .... 👄 .... ♡ ....

Popsicles or snow cones?

✌ .... ❀ .... 👄 .... 💘 ....

Coolest person to sign your yearbook

✌ .... ❀ .... 👄 .... 💘 ....

Love is: Complicated, Terrifying, or Amazing?

✌ .... ❀ .... 👄 .... 💘 ....

Ever gone away to **CAMP**?

✌ .... ❀ .... 👄 .... 💘 ....

Did you love it or **hate it**?

✌ .... ❀ .... 👄 .... 💘 ....

What saying would you like to put on a T-shirt?

✌ .... ❀ .... 👄 .... 💘 ....

Someone in your family you never got to meet but you'd like to

✌ .... ❀ .... 👄 .... 💘 ....

Last time you **freaked out**, it was because of …

✌ .... ❀ .... 👄 .... 💘 ....

Fav type of **puppy**

✌ .... ❀ .... 👄 .... 💘 ....

Burgers or **hotdogs**?

✌ .... ❀ .... 👄 .... 💘 ....

Ever give your friends *roses* on *Valentine's Day*?

Ⓥ .... ✿ .... 👄 .... ♡ ....

How do you **help a friend** who's having a **bad day**?

Ⓥ .... ✿ .... 👄 .... ♡ ....

TALKATIVE or QUIET?

Ⓥ .... ✿ .... 👄 .... ♡ ....

Ever liked a guy with a girlfriend?

Ⓥ .... ✿ .... 👄 .... ♡ ....

Do you have to take **summer school**?

Ⓥ .... ✿ .... 👄 .... ♡ ....

One word to describe *pimples*

Ⓥ .... ✿ .... 👄 .... ♡ ....

Do you sing in the shower?

Ⓥ .... ✿ .... 👄 .... ♡ ....

Fav **pop star**

Ⓥ .... ✿ .... 👄 .... ♡ ....

Ever stood up for someone being bullied?

Ⓥ .... ✿ .... 👄 .... ♡ ....

Your parents say you're **switching schools**: Cry or Get excited?

Ⓥ .... ✿ .... 👄 .... ♡ ....

Do you **get along better** with your **mom** or **dad**?

✌ .... ✿ .... 👄 .... 💘 ....

Are you part of a **clique** at school?

✌ .... ✿ .... 👄 .... 💘 ....

Which one?

✌ .... ✿ .... 👄 .... 💘 ....

Your most **GENEROUS** friend

✌ .... ✿ .... 👄 .... 💘 ....

Patient or *fidgety*?

✌ .... ✿ .... 👄 .... 💘 ....

One word to describe your PɛRSONaL STYLɛ

✌ .... ✿ .... 👄 .... 💘 ....

YOU WISH YOU WERE: Taller, Thinner, Shorter, or More athletic?

✌ .... ✿ .... 👄 .... 💘 ....

Hair color you like **best** on a **guy**

✌ .... ✿ .... 👄 .... 💘 ....

One thing that saves your SaNITY

✌ .... ✿ .... 👄 .... 💘 ....

Most likely to *write* a **book**

✌ .... ✿ .... 👄 .... 💘 ....

Most likely to marry a **supermodel**

✌ .... ❀ .... 👄 .... 💘 ....

Most likely to be in **politics**

✌ .... ❀ .... 👄 .... 💘 ....

Most likely to be a *fashion designer*

✌ .... ❀ .... 👄 .... 💘 ....

Most likely to win a **gold medal** in the **Olympics**

✌ .... ❀ .... 👄 .... 💘 ....

Most likely to end up on **MTV**

✌ .... ❀ .... 👄 .... 💘 ....

Most likely to win the **Nobel Prize**

✌ .... ❀ .... 👄 .... 💘 ....

Most likely to have 10 kids

✌ .... ❀ .... 👄 .... 💘 ....

Most likely to **stay single** forever

✌ .... ❀ .... 👄 .... 💘 ....

Most likely to be a **celebrity**

✌ .... ❀ .... 👄 .... 💘 ....

Last question ... Did you have fun filling out this book?

✌ .... ❀ .... 👄 .... 💘 ....

Quiz:

Are You A Drama Queen?

1. You spot your friend's boyfriend at the mall with another girl. You:

a. Do nothing; the girl is probably just a friend.

b. Take a picture on your cell phone and text it to everyone you know. Cheater!

c. Call another friend to come help you follow them. This will be hot gossip on Monday.

....

2. You find out that a certain girl told everyone a really embarrassing story about you. You:

a. Ask to talk about it, then tell her how she hurt your feelings.

b. Start a rumor that she has halitosis.

c. Walk up to her at lunch and yell at her to mind her own business, in front of everyone.

....

3. Your writing teacher gives you a C on your paper. You:

a. Ask if you can meet with her after class to find out why you got the low grade.

b. Call her an idiot under your breath.

c. Start crying. People always feel bad if you cry.

....

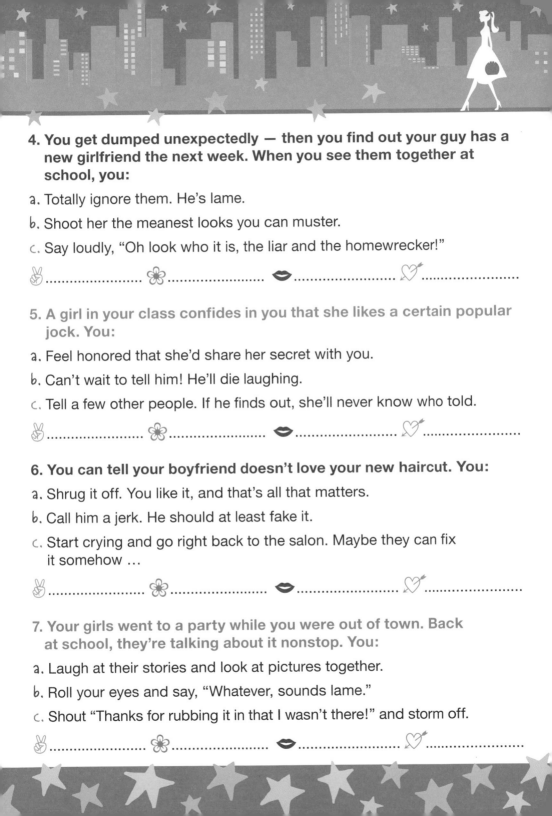

4. You get dumped unexpectedly — then you find out your guy has a new girlfriend the next week. When you see them together at school, you:

a. Totally ignore them. He's lame.

b. Shoot her the meanest looks you can muster.

c. Say loudly, "Oh look who it is, the liar and the homewrecker!"

✌ .... ❀ .... 👄 .... 💘 ....

5. A girl in your class confides in you that she likes a certain popular jock. You:

a. Feel honored that she'd share her secret with you.

b. Can't wait to tell him! He'll die laughing.

c. Tell a few other people. If he finds out, she'll never know who told.

✌ .... ❀ .... 👄 .... 💘 ....

6. You can tell your boyfriend doesn't love your new haircut. You:

a. Shrug it off. You like it, and that's all that matters.

b. Call him a jerk. He should at least fake it.

c. Start crying and go right back to the salon. Maybe they can fix it somehow …

✌ .... ❀ .... 👄 .... 💘 ....

7. Your girls went to a party while you were out of town. Back at school, they're talking about it nonstop. You:

a. Laugh at their stories and look at pictures together.

b. Roll your eyes and say, "Whatever, sounds lame."

c. Shout "Thanks for rubbing it in that I wasn't there!" and storm off.

✌ .... ❀ .... 👄 .... 💘 ....

8. Your shoe breaks in the middle of school. You:

a. Find a safety pin to fix it for the day.

b. Make your mom bring you another pair, right NOW.

c. Complain to everyone you see that day.

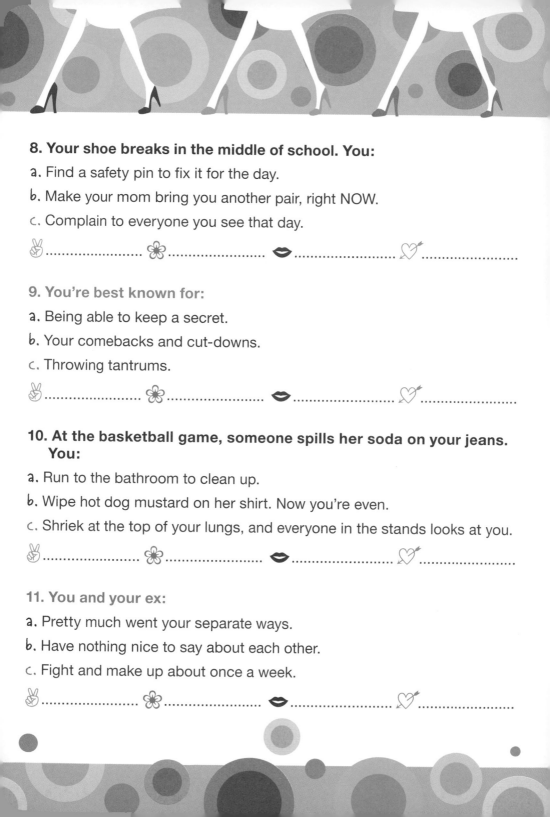 .... 🌸 .... 👄 .... 💘 ....

9. You're best known for:

a. Being able to keep a secret.

b. Your comebacks and cut-downs.

c. Throwing tantrums.

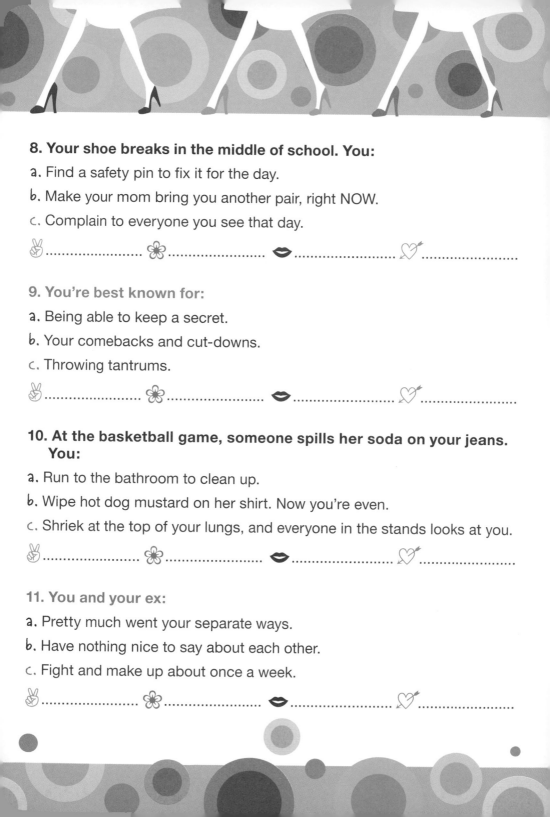 .... 🌸 .... 👄 .... 💘 ....

10. At the basketball game, someone spills her soda on your jeans. You:

a. Run to the bathroom to clean up.

b. Wipe hot dog mustard on her shirt. Now you're even.

c. Shriek at the top of your lungs, and everyone in the stands looks at you.

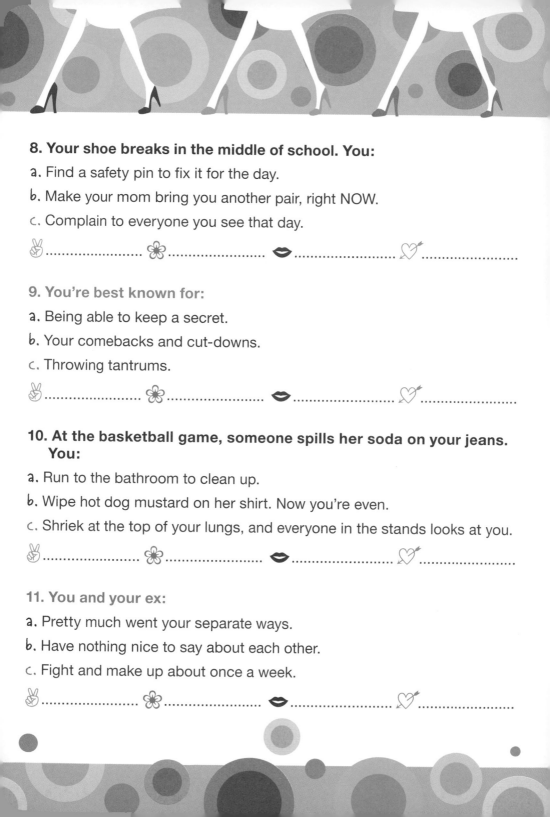 .... 🌸 .... 👄 .... 💘 ....

11. You and your ex:

a. Pretty much went your separate ways.

b. Have nothing nice to say about each other.

c. Fight and make up about once a week.

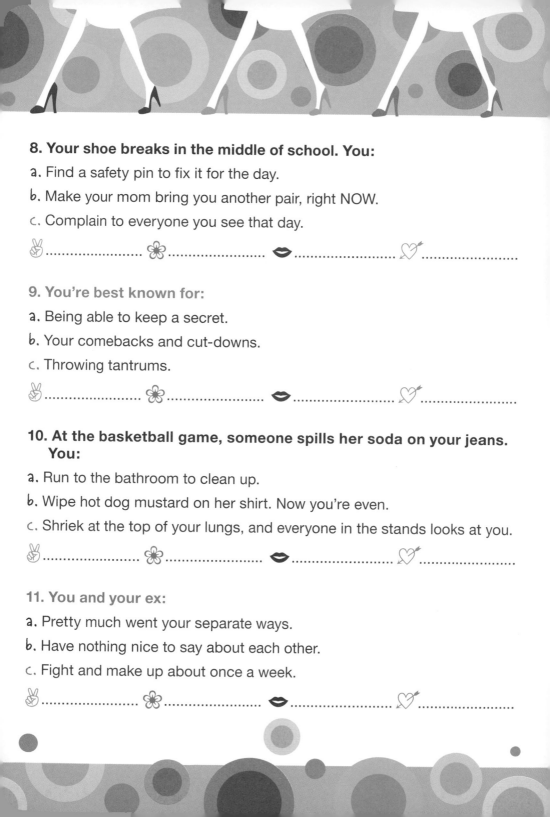 .... 🌸 .... 👄 .... 💘 ....

Mostly a's:

Chill Chick: Leave the drama to someone else! You're level-headed and know how to keep your cool. You realize that most things aren't worth getting upset over, and you try and find solutions when there's a mishap. Congrats — this makes you the kind of girl people like to hang out with, work with, and confide in.

Mostly b's:

Queen of Mean: Not only do you create a scene, but you're mean about it, too. Putting people down or making them feel stupid doesn't build you up or make you look important. Try not sweating the small stuff — most things are not worth freaking out over. People will have more respect for you if you keep your cool.

Mostly c's:

Drama-Rama: Part of the reason you love drama is that you enjoy being the center of attention — even at someone else's expense. However, you're wrong if you think drama is fun or cool; it's actually damaging to your reputation and friendships. No one wants to hang out with a girl who's a ticking bomb, so try taking a deep breath before you feel the need to draw attention to yourself.

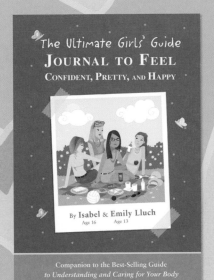

THE ULTIMATE GIRLS' GUIDE JOURNAL TO FEEL CONFIDENT, PRETTY, AND HAPPY

This companion journal to the best-selling title *The Ultimate Girls' Guide to Understanding and Caring for Your Body* gives girls a place to write down the thoughts and emotions that go with the changes of growing up. Fill-in-the-blank sections, quizzes, and checklists on every important topic in a preteen girl's life offers girls space for all their personal, private thoughts. Girls will be able to cope with the changes of puberty, as well as look and feel great!

Size: 5.5 x 8, 100 pp
ISBN-13: 978-1-934386-59-0
US $9.95/Concealed wire-o, Hardcover

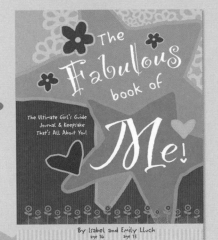

THE FABULOUS BOOK OF ME!

Who was your first kiss? What is the one thing you can't live without? Which classmate is your secret crush? The *Fabulous Book of Me* gives teen and preteen girls a unique opportunity to record their autobiography.

Journal space, quizzes, and photo pages for subjects like friends, family, school, crushes and love, style, personality, and dreams help girls create a treasured record of their emotions, friendships, hopes, and memories.

Size: 6.75" x 8.25", 100 pp
US $12.95/Concealed wire-o, Hardcover
ISBN-13: 978-1-934386-57-6

Join Isabel & Emily on Facebook.com

Best Friends Forever!!!!